Defending the
America's Cup

DEFENDING THE AMERICA'S CUP

EDITED BY ROBERT W. CARRICK AND STANLEY Z. ROSENFELD

NEW YORK   ALFRED A. KNOPF   1969

THIS IS A BORZOI BOOK,
PUBLISHED BY ALFRED A. KNOPF, INC.

First Edition

Library of Congress Catalog Card Number: 78–79336

Manufactured in the United States of America

Contents

Introduction

There have been a number of books written about the competition for the America's Cup. Some have been by yachting writers (including one of the undersigned), some by individuals directly involved in sailing one of the contending yachts. These were conscientious reports of the international races, chroniclings of events largely from one man's point of view. *Defending the America's Cup* is more a story of people than of events, told in the words of fifteen men intimately connected with *Intrepid,* the 1967 defender.

The text consists entirely of taped interviews with Syndicate members, the designer, the skipper, and some members of the crew. It tells the story of how a syndicate is born, how a fine design comes into being, and how the skipper selects his crew and makes them extensions of himself just as he becomes a part of his boat.

In recent years, as amateurs have replaced professional helmsmen and crews, the defense of the Cup has become a highly personal experience. To those who manned *Intrepid,* allegiance to the United States and to the New York Yacht Club was subordinated to their own personal sense of purpose. They were motivated by an insatiable love of sailing and by an awareness that Cup competition has an awesome place in the yachting world. So every man set his own standards of performance at nothing less than perfection. As a crew, their dedication was beyond words, and because of the kind of people they were, each man by fulfilling his primary responsibility to himself ultimately discharged his obligation to club and country.

As each man tells in his own words what he felt, how he related to the rest of the group, and how he performed his particular duties, we hope you will gain a unique understanding of what it is like to be "Defending the America's Cup."

Robert W. Carrick
Stanley Z. Rosenfeld

January, 1969

Spokesmen for INTREPID

Brief biographical notes on the fifteen people who have written this book through the medium of the tape recorder

EMIL MOSBACHER, JR., skipper of *Intrepid,* began to show his talent as a helmsman at the age of thirteen, when he won the Midget Championship of Long Island Sound. Four years later he took the Sound Junior Championship and then went on to win the Intercollegiate Sailing Championship for Dartmouth in 1941 and 1942.

In 1949 he steered the 6-Meter *Llanoria* to victory in the British American Cup team race at Cowes, England. The following year Bus began his remarkable conquest of the International One-Design Class. It was remarkable because in this class the men were quickly sorted from the boys by some of the best helmsmen in the east. But Bus took them on and won the class championship not once but eight years running. Along the way he came up with two Hipkins Trophies for the Men's Championship of Long Island Sound.

Intrepid's helmsman is not just a 'round-the-buoys' skipper. He has logged thousands of miles with the ocean racing fleet in all the major offshore events. He has made the passage to Bermuda four times. The year 1960 is typical of his blue-water activities: Southern Ocean Racing Conference, Storm Trysail Block Island Race, Bermuda Race, New York Yacht Club Cruise and the Vineyard Race. From time to time Bus has cruised for pleasure the Bahamas, the Florida Keys, Cape Cod and the Greek Islands.

Mosbacher's experience in 12-Meter sailing goes back to 1958 when America's Cup competition was revived for the first time since the "J" boats raced in 1937.

In the trials prior to the international competition, Bus sailed the nineteen-year-old *Vim* against three brand-new boats, *Columbia, Easterner,* and *Weatherly.* John Matthews had *Vim* in fine shape and Mosbacher came awesomely close to winning the defender's assignment from *Columbia.* In 1960 and 1961 he spent some time at the helm of *Easterner* and in 1962, he coaxed, cajoled, and drove *Weatherly* through the selection trials and successfully defended the Cup against *Gretel.* By the time he took the multi-wheel helm of *Intrepid,* Bus had accumu-lated more racing hours in a 12-Meter than anyone else in the world.

Despite his devotion to sailing, he is a successful businessman, an ardent fund-raiser for Choate and Dartmouth, and a trustee of a hospital and a bank. He has served on the U.S. Olympic Yachting Committee and on the Mayor's Sports Commission and has been Co-chairman of the American Red Cross Fund Raising Drive in New York City. Early in 1969 he was appointed Chief of Protocol with the Department of State.

EMIL MOSBACHER, SR., father of *Intrepid*'s skipper, is a messenger-boy-to-million-aire product of Wall Street. His interest in sailing and in raising sailors is reflected in his own words in the chapter on "The Skipper."

OLIN J. STEPHENS II, designer of *Intrepid,* is a sports car buff and a competent painter and photographer in addition to being one of the foremost naval archi-tects in the world. He has achieved this stature with a minimum of technical training. He left Massachusetts Institute of Technology in his freshman year because he "wasn't happy with what he was doing." At the age of twenty, he became associated with Drake Sparkman, and a year later, in 1929, they incor-porated the design and brokerage firm that bears their names.

Stephens says that Ken Davidson of Stevens Institute in Hoboken was an im-portant influence in developing his design ideas, which have had a marked impact on the yachting world. In 1931 he designed *Dorade,* a fifty-two-foot ocean-racing yawl, the forerunner of a new breed of blue-water competitors. With his brother, Roderick, Jr., his father, Roderick, Sr., and a driving crew, Olin won the Trans-Atlantic race from Newport to Plymouth, England, by a margin of three days over larger boats such as *Landfall* and *Highland Light.* The race from Newport to Bergen, Norway, in 1935 was won by *Stormy Weather,* another new Stephens design. The Bermuda Race was also a proving ground. He did the lines for *Edlu,* which won in 1934, and for *Baruna,* the seventy-two-foot yawl on which he was navigator, which won the '38 race.

For the Cup defense in 1937, Stephens collaborated with veteran designer W. Starling Burgess to create Harold Vanderbilt's 135-foot *Ranger,* the last and greatest of the "J" boats. Apparently, both designers prepared lines for the boat . and four models were made and tank-tested at Stevens Institute, but whose lines were actually used for *Ranger* has been a secret well kept by Messrs. Vanderbilt and Stephens. Olin served as relief helmsman on the '37 Cup defender.

His first 12-Meter, *Vim,* was designed for Harold Vanderbilt in 1939. The boat was extensively campaigned in England and proved considerably faster than the British Twelves of that period. Perhaps the handwriting was already on the wall. *Vim* was still going strong in 1958, but in that year Stephens designed

Columbia. For the first time he was in competition with himself. His newest Twelve won the defense assignment and the Cup Races and set the pattern for years to come. He didn't design a new boat for the 1962 series, but produced *Constellation* in 1964. By then *Columbia* had become an "old" boat and offered little competition for his new contender. In '67 three of the four candidates for the defense were Stephens's designs: *Columbia, Constellation,* and *Intrepid.* History repeated itself—the new design was clearly superior, proving Olin's firm conviction that there are still many ways of improving 12-Meter design.

He has also produced numerous class designs: many years ago, the New York 32's, and more recently boats ranging from the 13-foot Blue Jays to the 42-foot Comanche, the largest of several classes of fiberglass sloops designed for the Chris-Craft Corporation.

Stephens's achievements over the years are written boldly in the record books, which contain such illustrious names as *Finisterre* and *Bolero* and many others.

WILLIAM J. STRAWBRIDGE, *Intrepid* Syndicate Manager, began sailing as a young-ster out of Northeast Harbor, Maine, where his family had a summer home. At the age of twenty-two, he bought *Istalena,* a Class M sloop with an overall length of 88 feet. Strawbridge raced her out of Larchmont for a season and then commissioned L. Francis Herreshoff to design the 12-Meter yacht *Mitena.* She was a handsome boat, but not a match for the group of Twelves that were very active in the 1930's. He campaigned *Mitena* for several years, then got married and gave up big-boat racing. He continued sailing in the fleet of International One-Designs at Northeast Harbor, where he was Commodore of the Yacht Club for a number of years.

Quiet and introspective, Bill has always been extremely interested in yacht design, of which he has more than the average sailor's knowledge; consequently, he had a spontaneous rapport with Olin Stephens. The formation of the *Intrepid* Syndicate was a natural outgrowth of this association.

J. BURR BARTRAM, Syndicate member, was born in the building that is now the Black Rock Yacht Club and has spent most of his life on or near the water. For generations his family owned a packet line with boats plying between New York and Savannah. They operated the *Exact,* the *Excel,* and the *Annie Taylor.*

Burr started sailing in the family's 18-foot knockabout sloop. He crewed on a variety of racing boats ranging in size from Atlantics to New York 40's. When he was twenty-one years old, his father gave him a Seawanhaka Schooner. Eventually he made the transition from sail to power and built a handsome motorsailer, the *Exact.* He subsequently owned many powerboats of the same name.

He served as Commodore of the New York Yacht Club in 1957–58 and was on the America's Cup Committee to select the Defender in 1962. In 1967, as an organizing member of the *Intrepid* Syndicate, he watched the proceedings at-tentively from his 72-foot motor yacht, *Exact,* which was moored across the dock from *Intrepid* in Newport Shipyard.

Bartram was greatly admired by the *Intrepid* crew and on a layday in the middle of the Cup Races they paraded down the dock to present him with a mammoth birthday cake which Bizzy Monte-Sano had decorated with appropriate comments and ornaments.

HAROLD S. VANDERBILT, called Mike, Syndicate member and one of the great skippers in the history of yachting, successfully defended three challenges for the America's Cup in the golden age of the "J" boats. At the helm of *Enterprise* in 1930, he defeated *Shamrock V*, the last of Sir Thomas Lipton's five challengers. Four years later England almost took the Cup when T.O.M. Sopwith's blue-hulled *Endeavour* won the first two races from Vanderbilt in *Rainbow*. The Cup was in jeopardy for the first time. With an assist from the wily Sherman Hoyt, Vanderbilt came from behind to win the third race and then swept the next three contests to lock up the series four to two.

In 1937, the last year of big boats and professional crews, Sopwith's *Endeavour II* was no match for Vanderbilt's new defender, *Ranger*. He won four races by decisive margins ranging from $3\frac{1}{4}$ to $18\frac{1}{4}$ minutes.

In the early 1920's, when the keenest sailing competition was in schooners, he kept *Vagrant* in the forefront of the New York Yacht Club fleet. Later he raced the M Class sloop *Prestige* and in 1939 he campaigned the Stephens-designed 12-Meter *Vim* with distinction in this country and in England.

Vanderbilt didn't start with small boats and grow into larger ones, as is the case with most skippers today. He was a big-boat man who proved you can start at the top if you have what it takes to be a fine helmsman.

PATRICK E. HAGGERTY, Syndicate member, didn't really get hooked on sailing until he bought a Rhodes Vanguard in 1957 and began winning races with his family as crew. Before that he sailed sporadically in a Penguin and then a Chesapeake 20 while on active Navy duty in Washington, D.C., during World War II. Then he sailed a British Atalanta and a Rhodes ketch. At one time he owned *Andante*, a large motorsailor.

More recently, Pat built *Bay Bea*, a powerful ocean racer, which he has sailed in the Southern Ocean Racing Conference and in Trans-Atlantic Races. She is the successor to the first *Bay Bea*, built in 1963. An engineer-industrialist who is President of Texas Instruments Inc., he knows precisely why he likes sailing: the combination of companionship and coordinated group effort in racing. He became involved with the *Intrepid* Syndicate through his technical interest in yacht design and because his own competitive instincts were aroused by the challenge.

ROBERT W. MC CULLOUGH, skipper of *Constellation*, *Intrepid's* trial horse, has been sailing since he was six years old. His father, a member of the *Rainbow* Syndicate in 1934, was very interested in sailing and there was always a sailboat of some kind tied up to his family's dock in Stamford, Conn. Bob joined the Junior Sailing programs at Stamford and Larchmont, and one year represented Larchmont in the Midget Championships; he sailed a Star named *Constellation* and lost to Bus Mosbacher.

He grew up in Wee Scots and Stars and when he was nineteen he raced *Rattlesnake*, a 35-foot auxiliary sloop. Since 1963 he has been campaigning *Inverness*, a 46-foot yawl which has established a formidable record in the ocean-racing fleet. In 1965 *Inverness* was named the outstanding boat among the 155 participants in Block Island Race Week. In '66 McCullough captained the American Onion Patch Team and won first place in Class C in the Bermuda Race. He won the Cygnet Cup in 1968 for the best performance on the New York Yacht Club Cruise.

In round-the-buoys racing, McCullough has won championships in the Quincy Adams Class and for several years was Club Champion of the Riverside Yacht Club frostbite fleet. His experience in 12-Meters was limited to some crewing before World War II, but he became quickly acclimated to the helm of *Constellation*. After the Cup trials in 1967 McCullough beat *Columbia* and *American Eagle* in the Newport Cup Race for the Twelves that had been eliminated.

VICTOR A. ROMAGNA, Executive Officer of *Intrepid,* had the experience and seniority (he was forty-nine) to preside over the crew of the Defender with unusual equanimity. As a youngster sailing out of Port Washington, N.Y., he had the usual basic training in small boats on the Sound and quickly graduated to the ocean-racing fleet. He started crewing on Bermuda racers at the age of seventeen. By 1968 he had made fourteen passages to the Onion Patch. Vic has made three Trans-Atlantic Races, three Fastnet Races, and has participated in most of the distance races on the east coast.

He has been closely involved with the Twelves ever since they were revived for Cup competition in 1958. That year he was on the foredeck of *Columbia,* the Defender. The next two years he was on *Weatherly* just, as he says, learning more about 12-Meters. In the '62 Cup series Romagna was foredeck boss and Executive Officer on *Weatherly*. He avoided the 1964 Series and, of course, was cockpit crewman and Executive Officer for Bus in 1967, which he says was "a glorious year."

Romagna's knowledge of organization was valuable to *Intrepid;* it complemented Mosbacher's talent for decision-making. Vic had an overall view not only of a 12-Meter and its physical properties but of the emotional tolerances of the men working the boat, which he handled with a quick sense of humor and an even temper. Most sailors are eager to steer, but Romagna would rather be the best crew chief in the business.

GEORGE D. O'DAY, relief helmsman and cockpit crew, in 1960 was awarded the Herreshoff Trophy for his outstanding contribution to North American sailing. The award was made largely because George had won the Gold Medal in the 5.5 Meter Class in the '60 Olympics. He also won the Gold Medal in the 5.5's in the 1959 Pan American Games and the Mallory Trophy for the North American Men's Championship in 1957.

O'Day has a distinguished record as an individual competitor. He has won international class championships in the 110's, 210's, Fireflys, Jollyboats, and International 14's. In addition to collecting trophies, he has established a solid reputation as an expert in planing boats and as a downwind helmsman. He doesn't have quite the same touch sailing to windward and he admits it.

George started sailing in Marblehead's famous Brutal Beast Class. After cleaning up all the Junior honors at the Pleon Yacht Club, he graduated to the 16-

foot, dory-type Town Class and won the national championship in 1939. That same year he won the Interscholastic Championship in Tech dinghies. At Harvard, he played varsity football, captained the sailing team, and won the intercollegiate sailing championship in 1944.

In 1962 O'Day was co-helmsman on *Easterner* in the 12-Meter trials. He left this berth to join Mosbacher as an observer and adviser for *Weatherly* and ultimately came aboard her as relief helmsman for the Cup Races. He brought *Intrepid* his talents as a tactical sailor, and his long-standing friendship with Bus added to the cohesiveness of the team.

VINCENT (BIZZY) MONTE-SANO, JR., foredeck boss, got his first taste of sailing on his father's chartered S Class boat and in the family's knockabout dinghy. When he was about ten years old, he entered the Junior Sailing program at the Larchmont Yacht Club. His first instruction was in Dolphins, which Bizzy said "terrified" him. The program then changed to Blue Jays and when he was thirteen years old he got his own Blue Jay—on the condition that he maintain it and do all the work on the boat.

Monte-Sano moved up to a Lightning and sailed in the District, Atlantic Coast, and National Championships. Three more of the *Intrepid* crew, Billy Kelly, Bobby Connell, and Jory Hinman, served their apprenticeships in this class.

By the time he was twenty years old, Bizzy had crewed on three Bermuda Races, the first one in 1958 when he was sixteen. He sailed on Jakob Isbrandtsen's *Windrose* in the 1963 Trans-Atlantic and Fastnet Races, and did the Fastnet again in '65. He was a tailer in Mosbacher's crew when *Weatherly* defended the Cup in 1962.

On *Intrepid,* he ran a taut foredeck, but, more important, his effervescent sense of humor and spontaneous *bon mots* kept everyone on board relaxed and risible.

ROBERT A. CONNELL, foredeck crew, started out on his family's sailboat when he was two years old. At the age of nine he began racing Lightnings. When he was twenty, Bobby signed on *Malabar XIII* for his first Bermuda Race. That was in 1960, and he made the passage again in '62 and '66.

His 12-Meter experience goes back to 1961, when he sailed with Mosbacher on *Easterner* during an off-year for the Cup boats. Connell worked amidships on *Columbia* during her unsuccessful summer in the trials of '62, but he was aboard *Constellation* when she won the Cup against *Sovereign* in the '64 series.

Between times he sandwiched in three and a half years in the Navy, starting with Officers' Candidate School in Newport and including tours of duty in San Francisco and Norfolk. After his sabbatical on *Constellation,* he spent thirteen months in Vietnam.

WALLACE E. TOBIN, navigator, grew up on Martha's Vineyard, where most kids learn to sail before they can spell. Toby did both and then took a giant step and ended up as a tailer on *Columbia* when she defended the Cup in 1958. He sailed with Jakob Isbrandtsen in the Bermuda and Trans-Atlantic Races in '60 and crewed for him abroad in the Admiral's Cup Races the following year. In

1962 and '63 the U.S. Navy preempted his sailing time, but a new assignment sent him to the Naval Academy, where he was in charge of part of their sailing program. This enabled him to keep up his ocean racing. He made the '64 Bermuda Race and the Buenos Aires–Rio de Janiero, Annapolis–Newport, and Halifax races in 1965. He also went to England that year to race with Bill Snaith in the Admiral's Cup Series. The following year he took one of the Navy's sailing vessels in the Bermuda race and went on the Trans-Atlantic race to Sweden with Isbrandtsen.

At twenty-nine, Tobin was the oldest of the *Intrepid* crew (excluding cockpit personnel), which averaged twenty-five years of age. After graduating from Yale, he spent two years on a fellowship at Cambridge University in England and he retained a certain scholarly seriousness, balanced by a wry sense of humor.

DAVID K. ELWELL, JR., winch grinder, at twenty-one was the youngest member of the *Intrepid* crew. He began sailing in Blue Jays out of Huguenot Yacht Club in New Rochelle, N.Y., when he was about fourteen years old. The following year he bought his own Blue Jay and raced on the Sound until he was seventeen. Then he got a 110 Class sloop which he sailed until he began crewing on larger boats.

Dave was a twenty-year-old college junior when he wormed his way into a berth on Sumner (Huey) Long's *Ondine* for the 1966 Bermuda and Trans-Atlantic Races. In spite of his limited sailing background and lack of 12-Meter experience, he had the kind of intelligence and determination that led Mosbacher to try him out for a spot on *Intrepid*. Dave did the rest with guts and hard work.

WILLY CARSTENS, professional captain for *Intrepid* Syndicate, has been involved in the Cup races since he served on Harold Vanderbilt's first "J" boat, *Enterprise*, in 1930. He sailed on *Rainbow* in 1934 and became mate on *Ranger* in 1937. In those days, he recalls, sailors got ninety dollars a month and slept on board. There was extra money for racing and a bonus if the boat was selected. Willy was on *Vim* when Vanderbilt campaigned the 12-Meter in England. He stayed with the boat when she was sold to John Matthews and was on board when Mosbacher sailed her in 1958. The boat was sold to the Australians and Carstens was with her for a while down under.

One of the old school of Scandinavian professionals, he has spent most of the last forty years maintaining fine yachts in shipshape and Bristol fashion, and that is what he and another professional, Walter Armstrong, did for *Intrepid* and her tender, *Mary Poppins*.

Defending the America's Cup

The Syndicate   1

BILL STRAWBRIDGE: The *Intrepid* [1] Syndicate evolved out of my interest in 12-Meters—it goes back to the 1930's. At that time I commissioned Francis Herreshoff to design *Mitena* for me. She was a pretty boat but not very fast. I raced her a couple of years. Then I got married and gave up big-boat racing. I got interested in the Twelves again in 1964, but not as a racing participant. I was trying to get my son Norris into the *American Eagle* operation, so I went to see Bill Luders, who had designed a new Twelve. He said he might be able to give Norris a job on her syndicate's power boat. He also mentioned that the boat wasn't really a proper tender. Well, I said, I had a pretty good boat and I might do the job. Right away quick, Bill said, "You're on." So I fell into that job and stuck with the *Eagle* through the summer.

Toward the end of the Cup trials, the *Eagle* Syndicate was having trouble. You always do when a boat starts to lose. So I became involved in some inside politics. Perhaps I opened my mouth more than I should, but what I said seemed to work and helped steer around a few problems with the afterguard. I guess Olin heard about this. He had lunch with me in Newport after the '64 Cup Races and he said, "I understand you've gotten interested in this America's Cup business. If there's anything I can do to help you in the future, don't hesitate to call me."

[1] Historic name of U.S. Navy ships dating back to the small vessel commanded by Stephen Decatur, which entered Tripoli harbor in 1804 and set fire to the captured American frigate *Philadelphia*.

Around February of 1965 I came to New York, not to see Olin in particular, but I thought I'd just drop in on him. We talked about the Twelves and seemed to have a lot of ideas in common. One thing led to another and I said I thought it was silly the way the whole thing had been done in '64. Two boats were built on a crash program and it cost a lot more money than I thought it should have. Properly run, properly organized, it could be a much easier operation and less expensive. Why wouldn't it be a good idea to get started on the 1967 Cup Defender right now? I said I'd pay for the design work if he'd get started on it.

Olin said he'd been approached by some people in Detroit who wanted to build a boat, but that he didn't have to commit himself until April. We talked a little further and I asked him who would be the best man to sail the boat if we went ahead with it. Immediately Olin said, "Bus Mosbacher."

I said I'd see what I could do. This meant I had to have money raised and some kind of a commitment from Bus by the first of April so Olin wouldn't have to sign up with the Detroit gang. I didn't have the slightest idea where to begin, but I knew if you were trying to raise money, you'd better have something to sell. So I went around to Bus right away and asked him if he'd be interested. He said he was very flattered but he couldn't commit himself then.

BUS MOSBACHER: Bill came to me and talked about '67. I had never had the opportunity to be involved with a boat that was being built right from the word go. It would mean sailing Olin's new Twelve and working with him from the beginning. But in all conscience, I didn't see how I could fully commit myself at that time. I really didn't think I was going to do it.

BILL STRAWBRIDGE: On the first of April, I had to tell Olin that I hadn't made much progress. Bus seemed interested but that was as far as it went. Then I went down to Hobe Sound to spend a week with Burr Bartram. Burr asked me what I was doing with the 12-Meter deal. I said not very much because Bus can't commit himself now and Olin is naturally reluctant to go ahead until he knows I have a helmsman and some promise of a syndicate.

Well, Burr got pretty excited about the idea and said he'd participate if I could line up some other people. We got talking about the kind and size of syndicate we should have. We both agreed it should be as small as possible, maybe five or six members. From talking with Olin and know-

4

Intrepid.

ing some of the *Eagle* figures we believed we could do the thing for about $700,000. That meant, say, four members at $150,000 each and two more at $50,000. One of our ideas was to have major Syndicate members pay in installments. If they put in fifty thousand in '65, another fifty when work started on the boat and another fifty in '67, it would ease the pain.

I was not to be a member of the Syndicate. My job was to manage it, although I would pay for some special items.

After my visit with Burr, I went home and without any real hope I called Jack Dorrance and said I'd like to come and see him. I don't imagine he had any idea what was up. I went over and started to tell him about it and, much to my surprise, he said he'd be delighted to take a share. So I called Burr and told him he'd better get a drink in his hand because, "You're in."

Things dragged on from then until around June. I was still trying to get Bus to commit himself a little more definitely, but he wouldn't. Finally Burr suggested having a meeting at his house. I said, "Fine— we'll get Olin and see if we can put a little heat on Bus."

Bus and Olin came to Burr's at ten in the morning, and I explained to Bus I was having a difficult time raising money because the men who might back the Syndicate wanted to know who would sail the boat, who would design it and how it would be managed and run. And I had to tell them I thought maybe Bus was willing to sail it but he'd made no commitment. "Olin can't commit himself until you say you'll sail the boat. You've stung him twice pretty badly and he doesn't want to find himself in competition with you again."

I had briefed Olin ahead of time and suggested he might try to influence Bus. So when Bus hesitated, Olin came right out, like he does so wonderfully at times like these, and said: "Bus, that's just not good enough for me. You've either got to say yes or no." Well, that put Bus over the hump and he said, "Of course, I can't actually commit myself because my father is ill and I have to run the business with my brother. If something happens to my father, I'd have to back out at the last minute."

I said to Bus, "All we really want you to say is that you're with us and not against us. In the spring of '67, if you find you can't do it, then at least we won't be racing against you and we'll try to get somebody else."

Well, that seemed to be good enough for everybody. It put Olin in the clear, although by this time it appeared that the Detroit effort was not going to materialize anyway.

BUS MOSBACHER: I don't think I ever officially said "Yes." I sort of backed into it, I guess. Even *after* the Cup Races, in the spring of 1968, one day I told my wife Pat that I was having lunch with Bill Strawbridge, and she said, "Are you finally going to come out and tell him you'll sail *Intrepid?*"

OLIN STEPHENS: Before leaving Newport in '64, I had a preliminary talk with Straw. Then, in January or maybe February of '65, three interested people came along, all at about the same time. Straw spoke to me and said he was really serious about a new boat and had gotten together the nucleus of a syndicate. Then within two or three days I heard from both Pat Dougan in California and Jack Anderson in Detroit. They both were interested in building new Twelves.

This was something of a dilemma. I wasn't sure whether I should do more than one boat or not. However, Straw had come first with a firm proposal and the Syndicate sounded very attractive and well set up. They had a rather cagy, tentative commitment from Bus, so I said I'd do the work.

BILL STRAWBRIDGE: Through the summer nothing much was done although we did begin tank testing. In the fall we had a meeting at the Racquet Club with the New York Yacht Club's Commodore, Percy Chubb and Burr and Jack Dorrance and Olin. We wanted to get help on names of people that might be approached. Things dragged on a bit. Finally somebody said, "Let's try Mike Vanderbilt." So I called Mike on the phone. I said we hadn't seen each other in a long time and I'd like to come up and talk with him. And he said, "That's right, Bill, the last time I saw you was the day you sailed on *Ranger* with me and the mast came out of your boat. I suppose you want me to join your syndicate." And I said yes. Then he asked, "When do you want to come up, right now?" I said, "No, I can't come right now." He said, "How about tomorrow?" I think this was on Thursday and the next day was Friday, not such a convenient day for me, but since Mike was obviously quite interested, I said, "I'll come up tomorrow."

So I quickly got Olin and Bus on the phone. Friday wasn't good for any of us. I had planned to go to Maryland on Saturday to shoot with Harry Sears, the head of the *Columbia* Syndicate in '58, Olin wanted to go to his place in Sheffield, Massachusetts, and Bus wanted to do something with his boys. Anyway, we all canceled everything and went up to Mike's and chatted about the Syndicate and he said, "Yes, I'll be glad to give whatever anybody else is giving. You can count me in." That gave us three men and put us halfway there, so we were ready to go. We could let contracts and begin all the other things we had to get into.

Things began to roll slowly. We were trying to get two more Syndicate members. Burr said, "I'll speak to my sister, Eleanor Radley."

I asked Olin if he knew of anybody. We were looking for western people and we thought we could pull some money out of Texas or some place like that. We had called just about everybody on the east coast and weren't getting anywhere. Then Olin suggested Pat Haggerty. I wrote him a letter and said I understood he might be interested in joining a 12-Meter syndicate. Pat came east and we talked with him in Olin's office. He said he'd let us know, but we didn't hear from him for a long time.

Finally Pat came in and that made four subscriptions of $150,000. About the same time Eleanor Radley made her contribution. Then, with some help from Burr, Gill Verney joined us. That gave us the necessary $700,000.

It took about eight months to put it all together because we had to be careful how we made our approaches. It wasn't like raising money for a charity, where you walked in hat in hand and said it's tax deductible. You had to find someone that was involved and not just a casual observer. And there were a lot of people who would have liked to be members of the Syndicate but who just couldn't put up that much money. We wanted to keep it small because the people who had been in the *Eagle* and *Constellation* Syndicates had very little satisfaction out of them. The big boys felt the little boys were getting all the say and vice versa. Both these syndicates appeared to have been unhappy situations. We were very careful about whom we asked because we didn't want anyone in the Syndicate who would try to take over the organization and running of the boat. We turned down two or three people for just this reason.

As Syndicate manager, I had an unusually free hand in running the show. Jack Sparkman of Carter, Ledyard and Milburn drew up the agreement. It was pretty interesting. I said it looked to me as if he were drawing up a manager's contract for customers to sign. I thought it was much too strongly worded in my favor but he said that was the way it should be.

It was quite an agreement. It pretty well spelled out what the manager was to do; it gave me carte blanche to run things. No one could join the Syndicate without the approval of the manager. I think the only sticky thing it said was that there must be unanimous approval of all Syndicate members, or maybe it was two thirds, before they could get rid of the manager.

We didn't have too many Syndicate meetings—only when we wanted money. When things began to jell, I got out progress reports and gave financial statements. I was determined to do that, because I understood some members of the '64 syndicates didn't have any idea where their money was going. I had my secretary keep our books. It wasn't that difficult.

Early in the game Bob McCullough came to us and said he had an option to charter *Constellation,* which had been sold abroad to a French Syndicate headed by Baron Marcel Bich. Bob wanted to know if the *Intrepid* Syndicate would be interested in taking this on. We thought it over and decided it would be wonderful. After our people had put up a lot of money, suppose something happened to the new boat? Somebody could run into it and sink it in the middle of Long Island Sound.

So we invited Peter Goomans, Baron Bich's associate, to lunch one day. He haggled a bit with us but we offered him $25,000 and he took it. We picked up the boat months later and she was in awful shape. We couldn't even get the rigging on her, it was so rusted. I figured another $25,000 would pull her through the summer with new sails and new gear. If the new boat was better, we could put *Constellation* away in July. As it turned out, we spent a lot more than we planned, but she was tremendously useful as a measuring stick for *Intrepid* and also we could keep a second crew in top shape. The America's Cup Committee had the heat on us all the time because they wanted four boats to even up the pairings for the trials. So we kept *Connie* going until she was eliminated.

BURR BARTRAM: I think it all began in the fall of '64. Bill Strawbridge was down shooting with Harry Sears and they got talking about the Twelves and Harry said he was interested. Later Bill came down to see me and I said I'd go along with it if he could get some other people. Eventually Harry decided he'd rather stay on the Cup Committee than join the Syndicate.

I was enthusiastic about the idea. I had been on the New York Yacht Club America's Cup Committee in '62. In '64 I couldn't afford to join a syndicate because I had just built a new boat, but I offered it to the Committee for observation, so I was involved with that series. I think the Cup is pretty sacred to people who like boats and I was happy to be helping defend it once again in '67.

The whole thing is just fascinating. I think it's the one trophy the country has that would be a shame to let out of our hands if there's any human way to keep it. I don't think it's a waste of money. Certainly it is not a business venture by any means—I guess maybe some people go into it with the idea of getting publicity or renown, or whatever the word is. I don't think anyone in our Syndicate had that idea. They just wanted to keep the Cup here. I'll grant you it's expensive and I suppose we were open to criticism for spending the money. On the other hand, our Syndicate people have given a great deal to charity—probably to more worthy causes than this. As far as I'm concerned, though, this was a good cause. It means something to the sporting world and we've added to the knowledge of new practices and designs and sails and rigging.

Somewhere along the line when we saw what the cost was really going to be, we realized we were going to have to have more money. It became increasingly embarrassing to go back to the Syndicate again and again. So we devised the idea of getting in some more people who were not Syndicate members but just contributors. Much to my surprise, it was quite successful. I think that out of eleven letters I wrote, we had nine favorable replies.

HAROLD VANDERBILT: I joined the Syndicate because I was as determined as ever to keep the Cup in the United States. For anyone interested in yacht racing, the defense of the America's Cup is indeed a personal challenge.

PAT HAGGERTY: It took me six months to really make up my mind to join the Syndicate. Living as far away as I did and being so short of time, I wasn't sure I could participate in the program. They asked me in the fall of '65 and it wasn't until about March of '66 that I finally decided to call Bill Strawbridge. I had been approached by two other syndicates. Charley Morgan, a designer and racing skipper, tried to put one together, and a Great Lakes group was working on the idea. I refused both, but neither had really reached the point of "Will you or won't you?"

I suppose I got involved for a variety of reasons. Everyone interested in sailing is conscious of the Twelves and their importance, but the biggest reason was my association with Olin. He is not only something of a genius but as fine a human being as I've ever known. He's humble and quiet-spoken and it's a pleasure to work with people like that.

My old *Bay Bea* once had some steering problems. In a Miami-Nassau Race we broached thirty-six times in one hour in the north Providence Channel with big following seas and the spinnaker up. So I went to Olin and we did some tank tests. Originally we had settled for a conventional or *Constellation*-type underbody. Now, in the correcting process we decided to go the other way with a kicker [2] and rudder aft. It's a welded aluminum boat, so we just performed a hysterectomy. I think *Bay Bea* was possibly the first boat Olin had tried this on and knowing he was working in the same direction on *Intrepid* made it doubly interesting.

I sailed *Bay Bea* in the next Southern Ocean Racing Conference series and she was clearly faster downwind and now completely controllable. Naturally, I was intrigued to see what this configuration would do on a 12-Meter. As an engineer, I can't help but be interested in research and development efforts aimed at improving yacht hulls and rigs. The actual amount of investigative money devoted to sailing is small alongside of what goes into electronics or aerodynamics or any of the modern technologies. Even though designing, building and racing a 12-Meter in an America's Cup series costs a lot of money, the proportion of it which goes into experimentation is chicken feed compared with what we spend on designing other kinds of complex equipment. At the same time it represents a very large proportion of all the research and development money spent on sailing. Consequently, I couldn't help being attracted to the Twelves, knowing that at least a moderate sum of money would go for tank testing the hull and on improving the rig, sails and other equipment. Obviously, this would benefit all competitive racing in displacement-type hulls.

You have to recognize that the America's Cup contest is an anachronism. In this day and age, it seems ridiculous to try so hard with a mechanism of movement which is so relatively slow. The efficiency of a sailboat in terms of distance covered is not very high. But maybe this is one of the exciting things about it.

There is no doubt that this is a country-to-country challenge, but it is peculiarly appropriate to our whole society that it is handled by a relatively small group of individuals as competitors and supporters.

Another reason I got into it—it seems to me that sailing is a special kind of sport, and America's Cup racing is its quintessence. There is an

[2] Skeglike appendage aft of the keel.

exquisiteness about the preparation, certainly in contemporary contests.

BILL STRAWBRIDGE: By the spring of '66 our financial problems were under control—at least temporarily. We'd been spending a lot of time tank-testing, but Olin had a hard time improving on the *Constellation* model. We'd hoped to start building the boat in August. When August came along, I was up in Maine and went down to see Olin at his house. He was getting a little bit stuck on the thing. He wasn't satisfied at all with what we had.

The original budget for tank-testing was about twenty-five thousand dollars and we'd already gone over thirty thousand. So I said, "Just try a couple more of the modifications that you've suggested and let me know how they come out."

About the first of September I went over and met Olin at the tank. We had one model that was pretty much like *Constellation* with a kicker added onto it. The other one was an *Intrepid* model with a cutaway keel and two rudders.[3] There wasn't much difference between them. We hemmed and hawed. There was something about the shape of the bow. We had done hardly any work on the bow because Olin had been experimenting with the stern all this time.

I said to Olin, "Just do this bow for me on one of the *Intrepid* models." There were two models, one a little heftier than the other. By geez, it wasn't much of a change at all but it jumped that model right up.

Of course, before that, we had arranged to charter *Constellation* and had also received permission from the Cup Committee to use her for the Syndicate boat if we wanted to. Since we already had a pretty darn good boat, I said to Olin "Let's go whole hog and shoot for the other one." So Olin made a few more changes in it and we got some results that really looked terrific. Olin was pleased and we went ahead and started building. We were then about two months behind schedule.

We had a terrible time getting some of the parts. All the extrusions for the masts had to be done to order by an aircraft manufacturer and we kept running into war priorities. Aircraft manufacturers weren't interested in doing any of it, and finally all the extrusions had to be run specially by the Alcoa Company in Pittsburgh. Burr worked this out through a friend of his at the company.

Olin was insistent that we get the titanium rig because it had a high strength-to-weight ratio and it saved so much weight, but this was a

[3] Steering rudder aft and tab on aft end of the keel.

tough one too. Jakob Isbrandtsen, an ocean racing skipper and contributor to the Syndicate, finally helped us out. He had a little company up in Buffalo that he thought could do the job. Don Wakeman of Sparkman & Stephens went up there and they said they could. This was another case of a company turning off part of their production to make special items for us and we paid tremendous premiums for it.

We contracted separately for everything: the boat, the masts, winches, rigging, booms, mast fittings, and sails. Even little parts like backstay sheaves and genoa tracks had separate contracts. Our running rigging was given to us by Columbian Rope Company.

Everything came hard, but the yard did a heck of a good job and the boat, in spite of a raise in wages, didn't cost any more than *Constellation*. Even so, I don't think she's quite as good structurally as *Connie*. Anyway, we were launched almost on schedule, maybe a week behind.

One of our biggest headaches was the tender, *Mary Poppins*. You can't get a good tender these days because most modern boats have chine-built hulls [4] that are wide and fat and go fast. We needed an old-fashioned, tugboat type—a boat with a little age. We found one up in Maine and got a surveyor who said she was all right. I knew there were some things not up to snuff but I thought she was perfectly good. When we brought her down to Minneford Yacht Yard at City Island, we found practically every frame from amidships aft was cracked and the fastenings weren't holding at all. We had to rebuild practically the whole darn boat, but we stuck with it because we had bought it and there wasn't anything else to do. We paid twelve thousand dollars for the boat and put about twenty thousand into her.

The business of housing a crew in Newport was a headache, too. We went up there two or three times and couldn't get anywhere. The people that own the big houses wanted fantastic sums for rent. One person asked fifty thousand dollars for three months. I was pretty fed up, so I went down to the Chamber of Commerce, and talked with a nice young fellow. "Look," I said, "it's all very fine for the Newport people to stick the Texas oil people when they come up here for the summer, but when you're sticking the people that are running America's Cup syndicates, you're killing the goose that laid the golden egg. It's not the only place to have these races and the people around Newport better wise up."

I don't know how much good it did, but within four or five days we found that Mrs. Whitehouse's place was for rent and we leased it for fifteen thousand dollars. We had to put in another five thousand or so

---

[4] The chine is the fore and aft line of the hull where side frames and bottom frames meet at an angle.

for showers and additional facilities, but it was a wonderful place and worked out very well.

In March of '67 I had to take up all the subscriptions I had originally intended to collect in July. Some time in April I took out a loan from a bank to pay the bills. Then we had a meeting of the Syndicate members and they all agreed to contribute a percentage beyond what they had put in so far.

This carried us through to about July. Then we wrote letters to maybe fifteen people asking them to become contributing members of the Syndicate. This brought in nine or ten people on a very modest scale and we were glad to have them. Just about that time Mike Vanderbilt wrote me a very nice letter saying that our operation was going very successfully so far, that we obviously had the best boat, and he was willing to put up whatever money we needed.

The Syndicate members were wonderful. They never interfered. They didn't want to bother us. I suppose it might have been different if *Intrepid* hadn't been doing so well, but these people were just there in Newport and that was that. I think Jack Dorrance and Gil Verney and Pat Haggerty sailed on the boat once or twice. Mike Vanderbilt came down to see her at the dock, but he wasn't well enough to go out.

BUS MOSBACHER: I was asked to be on the Syndicate's governing board but I didn't want to do anything but run the boat. The Syndicate agreed and that's the way it worked out. They were a unique group. Some of them were very knowledgeable sailors and while they were keenly interested in *Intrepid,* they stayed completely in the background. They never asked, "What in the world are you doing it *that* way for." In fact, they never came aboard unless they were invited— and that was embarrassing. Even when they were invited, they said, "Oh no, we don't want to get in your way." Occasionally, when they did come out, they'd get in the rumble seat [5] and sit there quietly. For us, it couldn't have been a nicer relationship.

BILL STRAWBRIDGE: I felt a tremendous responsibility to the Syndicate members to see that the thing was done right and to try to hold down the bills, which, of course, was just about impossible—everything gets out of hand towards the end of these operations. But I tried to put on the best show I could for them. My sense of responsibility to the New York Yacht Club was not all that great—I figured they should be darn glad we were there. That isn't the way they like to look at it, but it was

[5] Small cockpit aft of helmsman's station.

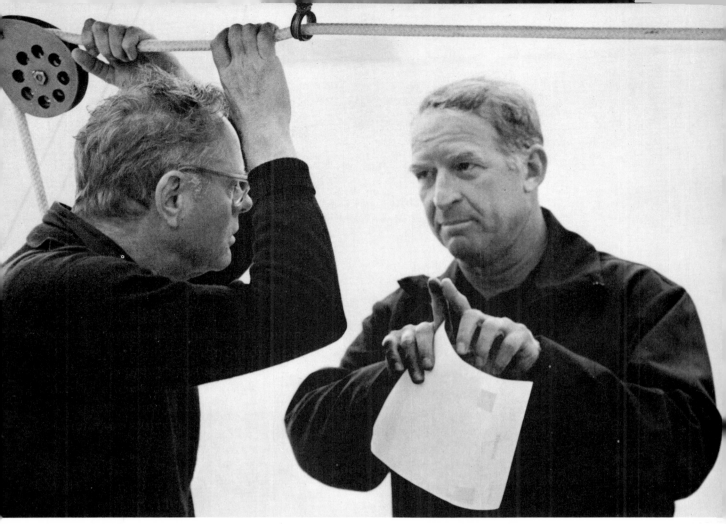

At the end of each day's sailing, Syndicate Manager Bill Strawbridge (left) and Skipper Bus Mosbacher conferred on ways to improve Intrepid's *performance.*

the Syndicate that was putting on the show.

It wasn't easy. We had all kinds of expenses and problems. I don't know what the exact coverage was for liability insurance but the premiums ran ten or twelve thousand dollars and on top of that we carried full racing coverage.

We went to the Newport Shipyard two years ahead of time. I told them we wanted all the land behind the dock, where we planned to put up a shed, but I never could get anything in writing from them. We really didn't know until the last minute whether we had it or not.

It's also funny, or maybe not so funny, that when *Connie* and *Intrepid* lost their masts on the New York cruise, we got a yard bill for three thousand dollars for *Constellation* and eight thousand for *Intrepid,* although the work had been practically the same on both. The insurance adjuster couldn't make head nor tail of it but he was damn nice and settled the claims satisfactorily.

Mary Poppins, Intrepid's tender, was a floating tool-shop and sail-locker as well as a towboat. Her radar came in handy when Intrepid continued practice sailing despite dense fog.

BILL
STRAWBRIDGE

Throughout the summer we were plagued with fog, but in spite of it *Intrepid* was out practicing or trial-racing almost every day. Olin and I watched from the bridge of *Mary Poppins*. We discussed how the boat was going but mostly looked at her sails. Then at the end of the day we'd compare how a sail looked to us off the boat and how it looked to those on *Intrepid*. We did an awful lot of experimenting with spinnakers. We found some of them were too big and we cut them down in size.

Olin carried a little black book and a camera and recorded everything. I never made any direct comments to Bus or the crew. Everything went through Olin.

OLIN STEPHENS: The Syndicate was quite remarkable. There was nothing I recommended that wasn't approved. And as the summer wore on, it seemed that the boat was so well equipped, so well sailed, and so well crewed that it didn't require any particular merit in design to get a winning combination. Straw in his own way made a greater contribution than many people realized.

The Design   2

OLIN STEPHENS: The authority to go ahead with designing *Intrepid* came along in the spring of 1965 and we started right off making a new model of *Constellation* as a yardstick for tank testing. Then we made a second model more or less according to ideas that had been working around in the back of my head for some time and this model, I might say, was a complete disaster. It was no good at all, so it showed I couldn't just go ahead on the basis of observations I made of *Constellation* in 1964.

Of course, design is sort of a perpetual-motion thinking process. There are some types of boats that feed into 12-Meter design just as the Twelves help other types of design. We had designed a boat in 1965 with a separate keel and rudder and, too, there was Dick Carter's *Rabbit*. Also there were European boats, the Giraglia-type French boats. These and the Cal 40's showed what could be done with this type of design.

I've always had a rough test of racing-boat design that is very simple. You just try to maximize the stability of the boat and minimize the wetted area. If you've got a boat with good stability and other things are more or less right, she's likely to be a pretty good boat in a breeze. If you can keep the wetted area down without sacrificing too much sail, she'll probably be a good boat in light weather. This is an oversimplification, but it's something I always keep in mind.

Then, of course, another question comes up: How short can you make your keel without having so little area of lateral resistance that you'll make a lot of leeway. Obviously, if your combination of hull form and keel doesn't compensate for the lateral forces supplied by the rig, the boat will just slide off sideways.

You can get some help on this leeway question from tank tests. Model-testing won't tell you everything about the leeway in a full-sized boat. It does give a good comparison between models but it still leaves you with some doubts. From my point of view, if I saw a model that made radically more leeway than another, I would be suspicious of it and would hesitate to go ahead.

Designer Olin Stephens contemplates one of the models for Intrepid *in the towing tank at Stevens Institute in Hoboken, N. J. He used a model of* Constellation *as a yardstick for thirty-five tests of seven different models. Testing cost the Syndicate more than $30,000.*

For example, in testing models for *Intrepid*, we had one that looked very good, except that it made more leeway than another model, which was a slightly modified *Constellation*. So this seemed like a logical application for the trim tab [1] because tests showed that with the tab, leeway could be reduced without increasing resistance. Conceivably that tab would improve performance to windward.

I had talked with people who had used the tab. Ted Hood had one on his One Ton Cup boat [2] and he thought it was very helpful. I asked Ted to check with Dick Carter to see if he would be willing to discuss the tab arrangement he had used on boats he had designed. Dick was agreeable and I talked with him about the tab. He was enthusiastic about it too, so we went ahead and tried it. In a sense, I guess this explains how we came up with two rudders on *Intrepid*.

So model testing is valuable. I think it's fair to say that if you're making model tests, you might try things you wouldn't put down if you knew the boat had to be built without tests. That doesn't mean there haven't been plenty of successful boats built without the tank. In fact, I'm sure that of all the boats we design less than ten per cent have model tests. With boats of the One Ton Cup type and the 5.5's, the cost of testing is relatively high compared with the cost of the boat, so in many cases it seems quite justified to go ahead and try out your ideas in the water rather than in the tank. Of course, some of these turn out well and some not so well. I think in making a big boat, an important boat, model-testing is sound insurance.

BILL STRAWBRIDGE: This testing business takes a lot of time, so I had Olin get started before the Syndicate really took shape. 12-Meter design has become pretty sophisticated, so all you're looking for is an improvement of a few seconds a mile and the tank gives some indication of this. It also gives some assurance that you aren't going to spend a great deal of money on a turkey.

OLIN STEPHENS: Models are made from lines done in our drafting office. Working on *Intrepid*, I believe we had over seven models. That's seven fundamentally different models, and on each of those there were some modifications. In the aggregate, I think there were about thirty-five different tests made. That would be an average of about five tests for each model, but some of them, one or two anyway, showed no promise at all and were left without alteration. On the more promising ones, we tried many minor changes to get the combination just right.

[1] Small secondary rudder hung on aft end of the keel or deadwood.
[2] A high-performance boat, designed to rate at twenty-two feet under the Royal Ocean Racing Club rule, that competes on a boat-for-boat basis without handicap.

Actually, this model-testing did pose dilemmas. It didn't run perfectly smoothly, and the fact that we ultimately came up with a good boat certainly doesn't prove that it is an easy or quick thing to do.

In fact, we came through the summer of 1966 with some nice improvements in the *Constellation* model which were achieved primarily through this kicker thing. But it was still just a modified *Constellation*.

A

B

With Intrepid *Stephens took a giant step in 12-Meter design. In 1964 he had gone to a concave shape for the aft end of* Constellation's *underbody (a). The kicker or "bustle" was added to this in 1967 (b).* Intrepid *was designed with a pronounced kicker, trim tab on the trailing edge of the keel, and a steering rudder (c). This combination was so successful the designer reduced the size of the rudder (d) to save on wetted surface.* Columbia *(background) has similarly shaped underbody but only one rudder.*

20

C

D

It was really only late in that summer that we got a boat that was better. To some extent this came about because a retest of the model we were about ready to go with didn't show up quite as well as another model that was more like *Intrepid,* which up to that point we had considered second best. We were hit with a dilemma when our best model dropped back a little and the second model came up a little—we wanted to get this thing settled.

So we decided to go to work with a different model. I don't know how logical that decision was, but at the time it seemed promising. We put a slightly different degree of displacement in the tuck area [3] or the so-called kicker, and rounded up [4] the bow a little bit and that was it. In a sense, every boat is a compromise that you're forced into by the calendar and the clock; you just have to go somewhere before you've really worked the design through, and we had promised to get the lines of the boat to the yard by the middle of September.

From the very beginning we had the idea of the snub bow. Straw liked it and I did too. In fact the first model we tested, the one that was so bad, had a somewhat snub bow. I wanted to keep the lower part of it close to the water without extending it too far and running up the weight.

Actually, the first model was not all bad. At one point, we cut it in half and fitted a stern like *Constellation's* to the snub bow and it didn't do badly. The exact profile and exact degree of snubbing we wound up with was pretty much arbitrarily determined after the testing. Models are made with somewhat lower freeboard and no sheer at all, so the snub business would hardly show.

We decided to go back to Minneford's. They had done a very fine job with *Constellation* and I felt we'd make no mistake to go there. Bob Derecktor was very anxious to build the boat and we did consider him seriously, but we simply had to make a choice on the basis of figures and so forth. Minneford's loftsman, Nels Halvorsen is, of course, very experienced in boats of this type. He's careful about checking the rule requirements: that there are no undue hollows, that the girths measure the way they ought to and that you get all the sail area you're entitled to. Poor Nels—he was really shocked at our bow. He tried very hard to lengthen it out.

While we were working on hull design, we tried, without complete success, to get a good start on various fittings. *Constellation* was started late and the whole process of design and construction was hurried. A lot of material was made on overtime, and some parts were made separately

[3] Area below waterline, aft of keel and adjacent to skeg or kicker.
[4] Rounded the sections forward.

Intrepid's *snub bow (foreground) was not as graceful as* Connie's *but was designed to save weight.*

that weren't altogether consistent; some parts we really didn't like but had to use. As a result, a fitting broke and *Connie* lost her mast in '64. So for *Intrepid* we resolved to get these rig fittings carefully designed and made up in good season. On the whole we were successful; although we overlooked some rather critical things having to do with spreader design, which was the reason for the mast trouble we had.

We went ahead with drawings of the rigging. This was taking a bit of a chance, because the strength of the rigging is dependent upon the stability of the boat. But we were pretty well able to assume that we would have a boat that was going to be a little bit more stable than *Constellation.* We allowed for extra stability and went ahead and planned rods for the rigging, clevises, and various parts of that sort. You know exactly what the mast height has to be on a 12-Meter so the rig is something you can start on before you settle the hull.

We decided to make the most of the properties of titanium because of its high strength-to-weight ratio. This was determined by a process of development as we got out drawings, estimates of costs, and quotations for this and that. Titanium is terribly expensive and the Syndicate had to think about that but they finally agreed to go ahead with most of it.

When it came to the deck layout, Bus and Vic Romagna had a big hand in the planning. I don't think my brother Rod or I would have come up with it independently. On the other hand I don't think they would have insisted upon it if they hadn't more or less allowed us to catch fire on the thing too.

BUS MOSBACHER: Sparkman & Stephens liked the *Constellation* deck layout. Vic and I didn't like it. It wasn't the kind of thing we wanted to work with. Among other things that layout called for not less than six or seven people, which meant twelve to sixteen hundred pounds of people-weight plus four or five hundred pounds of big winches, all back in the cockpit—and why? They all belonged in the center of the boat. We requested a rough drawing of the new boat. Olin gave it to us and we asked him to put a pencil mark where the center of the boat was. We had always understood this was the place where most of the weight should be and Olin said, "Yes, it should be—if you can get it there." So I said, "Okay, let's see what we can do."

Vic and I had thought for some time that we could get the weight and the winches below. One of the things I objected to about *Constellation's* layout was all the work that went on immediately in front of the helmsman. If you're trying to concentrate it's not helpful to have four or five guys moving in front of your face. Getting people forward and below gives the helmsman a clear view and ultimately I had a wonderful view looking forward from the wheel of *Intrepid.*

The deck layout on **Constellation** *forced crewmen to work directly in front of the helmsman. This not only obstructed the view but added significantly to topside weight.*

24

VIC ROMAGNA: I made the first sketch of the deck layout and Bus liked it. We sent it down to Sparkman & Stephens and they came up with another one which we didn't like. From the outset we were determined to have the winches below—our whole deck plan was predicated on this. Theirs was planned with winches on deck—it was just a replica of *Constellation*. We didn't see how we could sail with that. We wanted simplicity. We didn't know just what the coffee grinders would look like, but we had a pencil sketch of them down below. We also made sketches of where we wanted the hatches and where we wanted the tailers, who control the lines on the winch drums. S. & S. preferred one big forward hatch from which the spinnakers would come out, but I wanted one hatch on each side so there'd be no fouling of spinnakers. If the spinnaker pole is carried down the center, it fouls up the center hatch; with two hatches we were clear of the problem.

Bus wanted the steering station moved way forward. He hated being so far aft because he couldn't see as much—the angle of vision to the jib is poorer back there. So the whole cockpit was moved forward.

The idea of below-deck winches had been around for some time. We knew we had to get weight below, so okay put the damn things below and let's not fool around. We also wanted a bicycle arrangement but time was running out and we just settled for getting them below, period. I think that deck plan was the greatest thing we did.

*Intrepid's **uncluttered deck was planned by Mosbacher and Romagna. Pedestals that drive the big winch drums were mounted below to keep the weight low and centrally located.***

HAROLD VANDERBILT: We had winches below decks on *Enterprise* in 1930. Our headsails were trimmed down there. I had a mate sit in a hatchway to yell the orders below. Subsequently a rule change required accommodations below so the winches came up on deck on *Rainbow* and *Ranger*. Now the pendulum has swung and *Intrepid* is a racing machine like *Enterprise*.

OLIN STEPHENS: I think some credit for pedal-driven winches should go to Steve Colgate, who ended up sailing against us. I don't know Steve awfully well but I gather he has an interest in bicycle racing and it was he who came to Rod and urged that we test driving winches with pedals. We couldn't imagine anything using pedals on deck but we figured it wouldn't be too difficult to put something like a bicycle frame down below.

We had Graydon Smith in mind to make the winches and we went to him with this idea. He produced a device that could take either hand or leg power. It was sort of a hydraulic dynamometer affair and we made actual tests with it. We discovered that leg power was good for a much longer period but it was no more and no greater in short spurts than arm power. If anything, the arm power was faster, so we settled for that rather than getting too experimental.

BUS MOSBACHER: I think one of the most interesting things we did was to build a full-size mockup of the deck plan. It was set up in a shed at the old Nevins yard in City Island and it had hatches, working platforms, and everything that was on Vic's sketch. I liked the idea of the men working in hatches rather than on deck. They didn't have to worry about falling overboard and they were protected from getting whipped by sheets or things of that kind.

We never had to change a thing on *Intrepid* after she was built. Oh, I think we moved the sheet clamps about three inches but I don't think we moved a winch or anything else. That, of course, came out of hours and hours on that mockup at the yard.

VIC ROMAGNA: Bus effectively got a contained, quiet group who were pinned in hatches and stations below. They were out of sight and unable to get out of position. They *were* contained and quiet!

BUS MOSBACHER: There's a funny story about the deck plan. Vic and I worked this out with Olin. Rod Stephens didn't have a great deal to do

26

with *Intrepid* in the early stages. He sat in on meetings at Sparkman &
Stephens when he was here, but they were building some boats abroad
and he was out of the country quite a bit. So Rod came back from one
of his trips and Olin or Don Wakeman showed him our rough sketches
of what we wanted to do. Then Rod called me up and said he'd just
returned and had seen this deck layout and then he said, "We thought
Constellation was a pretty good layout, it worked very well for us, and I
think we all ought to sit down and discuss this plan of yours."

So I said sure and we set a date for four or five days later in my office.
Then I called Victor and said, "The fat's in the fire, sharpen your wits,
Rod's back and he doesn't think we're on the right track. So we've got a
meeting here Wednesday at ten o'clock and you'd better be over here at
nine because you and I are going to have to go over this."

Vic came in early and we spread out the plan on my desk and we
made all our arguments about why we liked this and why we liked that
and why we thought everything was good and why we didn't expect any
problems. Well, Rod came in. He had Olin and Don Wakeman with
him and we shook hands all around. Then Rod pulled out his copy of
the plans and spread them out in the desk and said, "You know, this
looks pretty good."

*Sparkman & Stephens favored one large sail hatch forward. Romagna held out for one
on each side of the boat. They were wet but more efficient for spinnaker handling.*

Vic and I felt like somebody had stuck a pin in us. Rod did make a few helpful suggestions, but he had no great argument with the plan. Olin did point out from time to time things he thought might give us trouble but he was always satisfied when Vic or I answered, "Yes, we know it's going to be hard but we'll make it work. We think the guys who are going to sail with us are smart enough, strong enough, quick enough, and capable enough to make it work. They know *Intrepid* is not a comfortable cruising boat and we're going to make it operate the way we want it to."

I think Rod was somewhat disturbed about the hatches. He was concerned about her being a very wet boat, which she was. But I kept getting back to the point that we were just day sailing, just afternoon sailing. We weren't going to Bermuda. If it blows over twenty-five or thirty they're not going to race us anyway. So OK, we pump or we get wet. We've pumped before.

OLIN STEPHENS: The low boom which we used was not one of our first thoughts. The sail plan was settled a little bit later and this tied in very well with the winches below decks because it would have been just about impossible to have pedestals [5] up there with the boom as low as we had it.

I must say the low boom was new to the 12-Meter class but not in any sense brand new. I think it had been working quite well in the 5.5's for some time. Actually, we arrived at the idea independently through

[5] Vertical housing for cranking mechanisms of coffee grinder winches.

The low boom—apparently resting on Mosbacher's shoulder—greatly increased the aspect ratio of the mainsail, a design feature neither the other American Twelves nor **Dame Pattie** *possessed.*

some theoretical aerodynamic people. While we were in the early design stages with *Intrepid,* we also were doing some work on a boat for United Aircraft. One of their consultants got talking about yachts and he said, "Why don't you put your boom right down on deck. If you can put your boom down so that the deck serves as sort of an end plate, it has the effect of virtually doubling the aspect ratio [6] of the sail."

Well, the aspect ratio of a sail has a lot to do with the so-called induced drag,[7] so that doubling the aspect ratio would cut the induced drag nearly in half and this would be quite an important gain. So we had Halsey Herreshoff do some tests at M.I.T. He tried putting strips under the boom, one that closed the gap to the deck halfway and one that closed it completely. Of course, he got more drive with the strips in place and the improvement seemed to be almost as much for the half closure [8] as the full closure. We obviously couldn't make a full closure, so we went for the half and it turned out to be a very desirable characteristic of the boat; it contributed to her performance.

It's something anyone could have done for the price of a new mainsail. Bus told me once he had heard that *Dame Pattie's* boom was going to be lowered but they never did. Must be they didn't agree with the idea. But I still like it. I know they are making a very low-cut jib in the Lightning Class and I understand that since they have used this, they have had to move the mast as far aft as the rules allow and their centerboard as far forward as they can to avoid having a lee helm. The low-cut jib was a good deal more powerful than earlier ones. So the idea seems to work.

BUS MOSBACHER: The low boom was something we had in mind from the beginning. It was part of the whole idea of putting the winches below decks. Early in the season, I guess there were times when people wondered whether UV, as the boys called him—Uncle Vicky—and I had not gone off our rockers. *Intrepid's* layout was pretty radically different from anything anybody had lived with before, but we thought it would work out and I believe it did. The problem of communications was made a little bit difficult because one or two things didn't come out quite the way they were supposed to. The pedestal winches were to have an interchange gear so that you could always crank the spinnaker from the forward pedestal under the hatch where the spinnaker trimmer was. Well, as it turned out, you couldn't interchange the winches and shift the drive to the forward one. So when the fellow grinding the sheet was on the aft winch he couldn't see, and instructions had to be

[6] The vertical extent of the sail in proportion to its horizontal measurement.
[7] Caused largely by turbulence at the masthead and under the boom.
[8] The aperture between the deck and experimental strips on the boom.

relayed. When the winches weren't cranking, you could hear Bizzy Monte-Sano call it. But when they got going, they made some noise and it was hard to stop them. That's when you saw stomping on the deck and the boys in the hatches leaning down giving hand signals. But communications worked out very well, I think, after midsummer.

Sailmaker Ted Hood was part of the Intrepid *team from the beginning. Sitting in front of the helmsman, he makes notes as headsails are tested early in the season.*

OLIN STEPHENS: We consulted Ted Hood early in the game. We said we wanted to work with him on sails. In fact, he was also discussed as helmsman. He and Bob Bavier agreed to help us if we needed them.

Ted is a busy guy, but when he got back from the One Ton Cup Races in '67, he spent quite a lot of time practice-sailing with us, checking out one sail and then another, mostly jibs and light sails. He developed the material for the floater, which was brand new—a very light fabric that was used for a couple of running sails; it proved very valuable. About halfway through the season, Ted developed a new pattern for his spinnakers. This was independent of Bus and me. He went into a more triangular spinnaker with less fullness at the head. The darn things didn't look so big, but they were certainly faster than the others. I think this was a real advance in the art, and was initiated and carried through by Ted. Our only part was in testing, proving that they were good.

Well, we finally got *Intrepid* launched on Friday, April 28. The first time we had her out a couple of days later it was very light. I had told Bus that with any luck at all we had a good boat in a breeze but that I had to admit to some reservations, even keep my fingers crossed, about how she would go in light air. But this was mainly due to the real

Skipper and designer discuss Intrepid's *initial performance on Long Island Sound.*

difficulty of evaluating the frictional resistance on model tests. A lot of people say it's very easy because there are certain formulas you can apply, but I don't think it's as simple as it's made out to be. I was very concerned about it so I was pleased the first day we took the boat out and put her on the wind in light air. Perhaps not right on the wind because we were sailing out from City Island towards Execution Light in a sort of southeasterly breeze. It was more of a reach than a beat but she seemed to move very nicely.

In the beginning, we were a little worried about her running. There didn't seem to be any big difference between *Constellation* and *Intrepid* off the wind. In the light air, I think it was a matter of spinnakers. The boats were very close and whichever had the right chute for the conditions seemed a little better.

But I was happy about her right straight along. I think it should be said that she had things going for her. It wasn't just the hull and it wasn't just the sails. The streamlined titanium rigging was an advantage, and the low boom, I presume, was an advantage. She was always in excellent shape and Bus, of course, had the pick of the crew that had been gathered together. With all those things she had the margin that was needed.

Another thing that was very nice about the boat—it wasn't just that she made a little bit better speed to windward than *Constellation* or the other competition—she would go no matter how you trimmed her. If you wanted to pinch her, you could pinch her, and if you wanted to rap her off, she was very fast on a close reach. This was very nice to have up your sleeve.

It was certainly valuable to us to have *Constellation* as a trial horse. It assured us that everything we had done, even down to minor items such as sail trim and sail-testing, was always being measured against a first-class standard. I believe it was ever so much better to have *Constellation* than the kind of boats we've had in the past. The new Twelves could sail circles around older boats like *Nyala* and *Nereus,* ex-*Northern Light,* so it was pretty hard to be sure one sail was better than another. But when the trial horse is a good, modern boat in its own right, then I think you can see much more quickly if anything is wrong. There wasn't much wrong with *Intrepid,* but certainly there were some sails that were better than others, so it was good to have a sensitive indicator.

After the kicker was added to *Constellation,* she was a fairly close match for *Intrepid,* except perhaps on the wind. Normally, footing the same, *Intrepid* would point a little higher; pointing the same, she could foot a little faster. She was just a little bit better but much of this was due to the helmsman and the trim of the sails. I don't say it was necessarily the design. I'd say it was a combination of design, helmsman, sails and so forth. When the two boats got together for practice, *Intrepid* almost always went faster; but it took a while and depended on who was steering. I was steering *Intrepid* one day and felt very badly because I couldn't get her ahead of *Constellation*. But Bus did.

Of course, off the wind in light air, *Intrepid* did not have much of an edge. *Constellation, Columbia,* and *Eagle* were pretty competitive here. I think this is partly because of *Intrepid's* high aspect-ratio rig. This enables her to function to windward very efficiently, but when you're off the wind, it's more a matter of sail area that counts and the sail area on *Intrepid* was small.

During the summer, especially as the Cup Races came closer, we heard a lot about *Dame Pattie* and her ability to point. Bus was concerned and I was, too. We talked about it and I said, "Well, if she points too high, just keep moving. If she gets on your lee bow and points high, just tack and give her a good rap full." I was quite confident that with those tactics *Intrepid* would be all right, and this proved to be true in the second race for the America's Cup.

Bus and I discussed the characteristics of the boat and the way to get the most out of her. We talked a good deal about the trim tab, and even now I don't think either one of us knows as much about it as we'd like to. We both wanted to win, and Bus found she went well with a certain trim on the tab. She balanced well and went well and he didn't do as much experimenting as I might have done perhaps if I'd been steering the boat.

BUS MOSBACHER: The tab and rudder and two wheels with a braking or clutching arrangement gave us a number of combinations. You could

The steering pedestal was originally designed with two wheels on the forward side so trim tab and rudder linkage could be adjusted by the cockpit crew. Mosbacher found it easier to handle this himself and the two wheels came off. Olin Stephens (left) with his brother, Rod.

set the tab at a given position or tie the tab and rudder together. Most of the time we synchronized them by putting pressure on the interlocking mechanism—a pressure I could override. Going to windward we had a consistent and constant amount of tab angle.[9] Then it became a matter of habit to adjust the tab every time you tacked. It was second nature, like flicking the turn signal on your car before you go around a corner. We varied the tab angle a bit, but basically Olin wanted to keep a 4° tab angle when we were beating so we trimmed the boat so it would balance with that angle.

OLIN STEPHENS: Tacking downwind was something Bus and I also discussed. I have always felt that finding the right point of sailing downwind in a light air was much more difficult than finding it going to windward. A very good sailor like Bus, an expert helmsman, can tell by the feel of the boat, by the seat of his pants, when he is making good speed to windward. You can sail too fine and know it because the boat stops and you can sail too wide and know the boat really isn't going much faster. Going downwind it is much more difficult, and the lighter the wind the higher you have to sail. We did work out some curves and turned them into simple rules for the degree by which you should sharpen up and the point to which you should bring the apparent wind [1] according to the wind speed and boat speed.

This was helpful, and was used by *Intrepid,* but I think it is a point that can be further investigated with the hope of doing even better in the future. The reason that my own technical ideas on this point haven't been applied as fully as I might like is because in match racing you have a tactical situation which does not permit you to tack downwind too far away from the other boat. However, with a crew like *Intrepid's,* you can jibe so efficiently that you can make short tacks and sail at the preferred angle. But your tactics, if you are ahead, are dictated by the other boat, so you can only carry this so far.

During our first practice sailing on the Sound, the crew didn't seem to think along technical lines. They didn't see or accept some of the structural limitations of a weight-saving design. They were all for giving the boat a test to the point of being a little bit rough—like jibing her without setting up the backstays in winds over twelve knots.

From June seventh on, I carried my black notebook every day on the tender. I don't think I am the most observant observer that ever watched a yacht race, but I was looking carefully for anything that promised to make the boats go better, particularly the rig and sails and their performance in different kinds of weather. I made a lot of notes

[9] The tab was offset about 4° to leeward of the center line of the boat.

[1] The direction of wind you sail by—produced by the effect of boat speed on the true wind.

Stephens believes the combination of many little things gives a boat its ultimate superiority. He added this pieplate to reduce turbulence caused by the trim tab.

about the racing which were more or less conscientiously put down without any confidence that it meant an awful lot, but sometimes I got a question or the fellows on the boat would ask me about a certain sail. Putting these things down with the time they occurred, enabled me to go back and check with the fellows on the boat.

Here are some comments about an early race with *Constellation:* "*Intrepid* rounded weather mark 1:35 ahead; after half hour changed spinnaker for new floater, holding high. *Intrepid* appears to be going better with floater. Sail looks good but *Intrepid* must have more wind, pulled well ahead of *Constellation.* Changed back to ¾-ounce all-around at 2:25 p.m. about half mile from 32A. *Constellation* sets cheater at 2:29, *Intrepid* follows at 2:30."

Of course, there are also notes of minor things to do at the yard: "Band on the boom, shorten bales for mainsheet boom blocks, lift for jockey pole, lower compass."

My notes on the loss of the first *Intrepid* mast are perhaps interesting: "The boat was on the wind, starboard tack, heeling angle about 30 degrees, main trimmed very flat, seized end of mainsheet right up to the block, boom in very low, 9-ounce genoa, high tension on halyard. We first heard a loud pop and looked aloft and after that the mast broke just below the lower spreaders." [2]

Fairly early in the season down at Newport we made a couple of changes on the boat. We added a sort of flat plate over the tab and a little later we reduced the area of the rudder and filled out the kicker area with a microballoon [3] substance.

[2] Rigid horizontal members projecting from the mast "spread" the shrouds that support the mast laterally.

[3] Minute synthetic particles that become a lightweight shaping (fairing) compound.

The purpose of the plate was to reduce turbulence created by the tab. We cut down the size of the rudder because we came to the conclusion that the boat could be steered easily with a smaller rudder used in conjunction with the tab. We made a small saving in wetted area which we felt helped just a little bit. It was one of those indefinable things, but it was in the right direction.

Throughout the summer Straw and I watched everything carefully from *Mary Poppins*—things like the setting of the mainsheet traveler [4] which you can see much better off the boat. You can watch the effect of this adjustment in regard to the twist [5] in the mainsail. If the traveler is set out a little bit to leeward and then the mainsail is trimmed very hard, this pulls the head of the sail in and reduces the twist. There is, in effect, a twist in the direction of the apparent wind between the lower and upper part of a sail and this can be related to the twist in the sail itself so as to get the most efficient drive out of the sail. Actually, *Intrepid* didn't have to adjust the traveler very much.

Aside from sails, we were concerned about some of the fittings, especially some of the titanium fittings and to some degree the welded aluminum fittings. This is strictly a technical point which has to do with the kind of material and the way it was welded. The titanium was used in two different forms, one annealed and the other heat-treated to get a little extra strength. The annealed parts were beautifully made. They caused us some worry by the failure of one or two but the annealed titanium was generally perfect as far as I'm concerned.

I think it was a mistake of our own to try to raise the strength a relatively small amount by heat treatment. As a result, some parts were very hard and brittle—like glass in a way. They were strong but wouldn't stand any misalignment or shock. One part that cracked without causing any particular failure was part of the halyard lock mechanism at the masthead. Then there were some internal tangs [6] of this type of material. None of these failed, but a corner of one base plate just broke off like a piece of glass. These items were remade for us by the Titanium Metals Corporation in their own laboratory. They put them together in their own way with their own recommended materials and they were fine. You could sense the difference: the remade parts, while extremely strong, had a reasonable amount of ductility and seemed almost soft.

We thought at first the original mast failure was due to failure of one of the titanium parts. When the second mast went, there was very little doubt about the reason. It was caused by the fitting we had designed to

[4] A horizontal athwartships fitting that can control how far the mainsheet lead "travels" from side to side of the boat.

[5] Deflection in the plane of the sail.

[6] Fittings by which rigging components are attached to the mast.

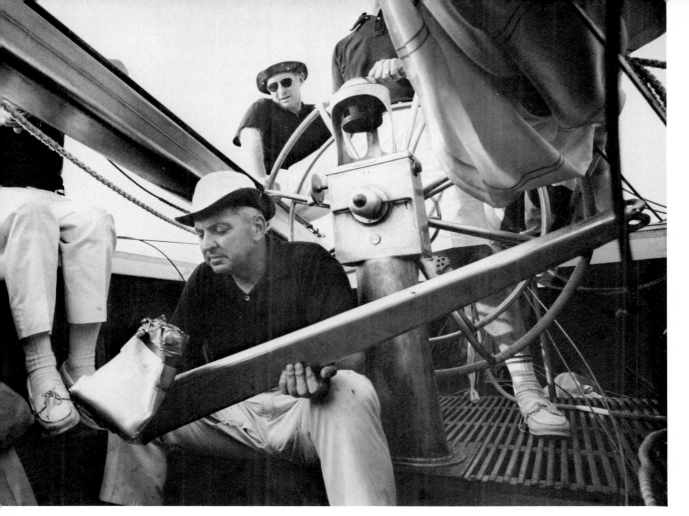

Since everything on Intrepid *was designed to save weight, the chance of failure was always present. During a practice sail on the Sound, she broke her mast. Vic Romagna examines the buckled inboard end of a spreader, later discovered to be cause of failure.*

slope the spreader down and forward. You see, the wind is assumed to be more or less in the plane of the water. When the boat heels over, the spreader will be more nearly lined up with the flow of the wind if it is lowered at the forward edge a bit. Now, when there is direct compression on the spreader, it creates a twisting load, which is bad enough; but as long as the spreader can withstand it, it's all right. Now, you start to pull your masthead aft to put a hook [7] in it and that pulls the outboard end of the spreader aft—the whole thing is pulled aft. Instead of having a straight load on the spreader, you are putting a bending load on the inboard end of it and it just folds right over.

Frankly, it wasn't a good design; in fact it was a bad design. It was the same thing we had on *Constellation* in '64, but there wasn't nearly so much effort put into bending the mast then as there was in '67. The fitting was a poor answer to the bending problem.

[7] A bend that produces more nearly perfect aerodynamic form in the sail.

37

To solve it, we simply made new spreaders that were heavier and stronger and no longer had that downward slope. They were flat, level with the plane of the water. I don't think they made any measurable difference in the performance of the boat, but I think the original idea was one of the little things you have to try. These little things are important; if you can get all of them working for you in the right direction, it will make the difference that counts. And if you have to, you can give up one or two of them.

When the mast went on *Intrepid,* I naturally felt very, very concerned and responsible. On the other hand, believing that it was clearly the fault of the spreader, I felt it wasn't anything that couldn't be solved. When you are working with such small margins, it is easy to go wrong.

Constellation lost her mast the same day *Intrepid* lost hers on the New York Yacht Club Cruise, but I think that was mainly because of unsuccessful welding of aluminum. Somebody extended her spreader. I

When the defender lost a second mast during the New York Yacht Club Cruise, Stephens redesigned the spreader, making it heavier and stronger. At Newport Shipyard, he carefully examines the new installation with Syndicate Manager Bill Strawbridge.

don't know when or how or where, but there was a piece about three or four inches long which was out of taper with the rest of the spreader. There was a little knuckle near the end and the thing just plain broke off, due probably to the sail hitting it when they jibed or something like that, rather than by the end load on the spreader.

When *Columbia* lost her mast on the West Coast early in '67, I believe from a semi-outsider's point of view, it was a clear case of bending the mast too far. That's probably why they didn't want to sail in a breeze of wind on the Cruise in '67—because of the extreme bend they had in the mast.

BUS MOSBACHER: When *Intrepid* lost her second spar, it was probably the most frustrating time of the summer. Frustrating not only because we lost that second spar but because we knew *Constellation* had lost hers the same day. Part of the frustration was that Olin, in my book, is the most capable designer and also one of the nicest people in the world. I don't know anything about spar construction, but just plain reacting as a businessman and facing consecutive failures, I arrived at a pretty definite conclusion that there was something basically unsound in the design.

Pat, Victor, Olin, and I drove back that night from Padanarum [8] to Newport in my car and I'm sure it was one of the longest drives for every one of us. I'm afraid I expressed myself just as definitely as I could —that I thought faulty design was the problem in my book and I didn't want to take the risk of hurting people any more. Equally important, were I on the Selection Committee I sure as hell wouldn't pick any boat that had a mast falling out every two weeks in a fifteen-knot breeze and a smooth sea. I for one would not be satisfied with another explanation that a clevis had slid out or that a titanium tang had fractured or something else. Previous failures had always been kissed off with something like that and I didn't think we could accept this any longer. A pretty basic investigation had better be made and they should go right back to the drawing boards with it—which, of course, they did.

The failure could not be laid at Olin's door really. He was not the rig designer as I understood it, but I think that at that particular point he got into it himself and from then on we had no trouble whatsoever. It was a frustrating thing and a very difficult time.

I'm delighted to be able to tell you that I was sitting on the deck to leeward when the boom dropped in my lap, and it hardly even hurt. That surprised me. I thought you'd probably get your legs chopped off.

[8] On Buzzards Bay, Mass., port of call on the New York Yacht Club Cruise.

BUS
MOSBACHER
The mast went over the side and missed. I was very lucky. It was a long, wet, uncomfortable tow back to Padanarum.

BILL STRAWBRIDGE: Olin was pretty upset when the second mast went out of *Intrepid*. He had tried to make everything as light as he could, but even in the beginning I don't think he was completely in favor of the way the spreaders were hooked onto the mast. I had another method of doing it, which I still think is better, but hell, that's only a matter of opinion anyway. There's no doubt about the trouble. I was right there and helped clean up the mess on *Intrepid*. I watched each piece of rigging and everything as it came off and was untangled. The only thing I could see was that it was the spreader at the inner end.

BIZZY MONTE-SANO: The night after we lost the mast I remember standing on the stairway at Eastbourne Lodge with Bus and Victor, Bob McCullough and Olin. Olin was on the stairs with the spreader in his hand and we were discussing it, looking at how the spreader had twisted. He had decided and we all agreed that the spreader had gone first and that was what had caused the failure. Olin had put the spreader down by this time and my wife, Mary, came down the stairs, picked up the spreader, and said, "Oh my goodness, that certainly is light, isn't it?" She had not meant anything and had not realized what we had said about the spreader.

Olin, quick as a wink, said, "Well, Mary, under other circumstances I would consider that a compliment." Well, at that everybody burst out laughing and a somber evening brightened just a bit.

OLIN STEPHENS: Obviously the summer was not without tensions. In '67 I was in a different position than I had been in before. Each of the other summers, each with a new boat I had designed, had a different pattern. *Columbia* in '58 was pretty much a close thing, a very close thing down to the very end. *Constellation* in '64 was a clear reversal. We had a boat we were all optimistic about in the beginning. She could sail circles around trial horses and I think we all were a little over-optimistic. In the early trials, *Connie* made a very poor showing but as the result of many different things she did come through in the end. With *Intrepid* we not only knew the potential was there, it was being delivered. And yet we felt, at least I did and I think Bus did, that in this front-runner position we might be tripped up. So all the way through both of us, and I hope rightly, avoided any real overconfidence.

In designing a racing machine you come very close to the edge of

40

safety. You have a lot of points of attachment, a whole string of beads, you might say, and any one might show a weakness. You know Murphy's Law: "If anything can go wrong, it will." We were in a position where we were doing very well, but we just couldn't help but be worried all the time. I know I was and Bus was. He felt it, too, and he was worried about *Dame Pattie* as well.

In the long run, everything worked out. I think Bus deserves tremendous credit. He is not just a helmsman, he is a great leader. He was certainly a cohesive force and his heterogeneous group in the end was very well integrated. I think the *Intrepid* crew had a much more emotional quality than any of the others I know. By comparison, *Constellation* in '64 had problems. She wasn't going in the beginning and they gradually got together a combination of good people and a good helmsman. Rod, I think, was primarily a good technical organizer and there were others who contributed. Eric Ridder, who didn't make things too easy in the beginning, graciously realized what his position had to be and turned over the helm to Bob Bavier. But this, to me, was all on a technical level. *Connie* was a fast boat and ultimately got going.

In some ways *Intrepid* was the same thing. She was a fast boat, too, but it was a different experience for me. Bus was responsible in an inspirational way for getting the group together and he's the kind of guy you really want to be associated with. *Constellation* is the type of boat I like to design, but *Intrepid* is the kind of effort I'm glad I was a part of.

CONSTRUCTION DETAILS

Looking aft from the bow, sail bins are located under the foredeck hatches.

Intrepid *had streamlined titanium rigging. Here, main shrouds are fastened to the chainplates.*

Intrepid's *mast-step. The jacking screw on the rider plate is used to adjust heel of mast. Rising diagonally on each side of the mast are the chainplate tie rods.*

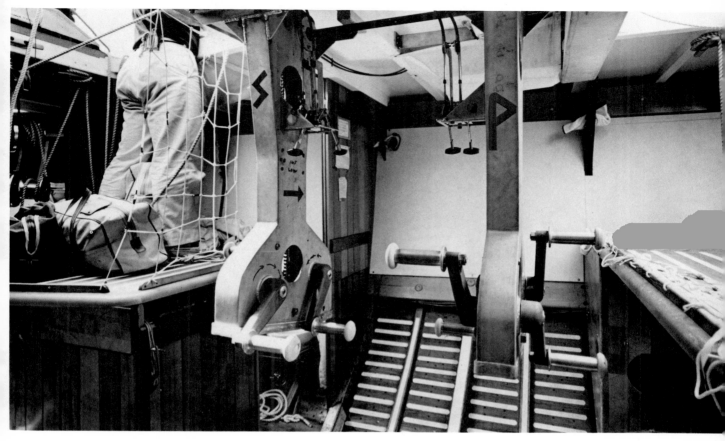

Coffee-grinder winches, located forward of the tailers' platform, are geared for three speeds.

Sheaves under the grating carry steering system cables that are painted to indicate rudder angle.

43

CONSTRUCTION
DETAILS

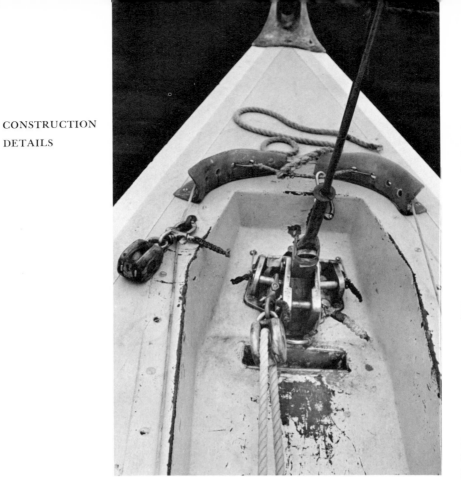

Left: Jib tack fitting is recessed to keep the foot of the genoa close to the deck for greater drive.

Right: Winch drums are set just forward of the tailers' platform. Handles are for smaller winches

Below: Genoa jib sheets run through the heavy turning block forward to coffee-grinder drum.

Small but powerful mainsheet winch is operated by crewman standing in the cockpit at right.

45

Intrepid's crew. From Bus Mosbacher (at the wheel) clockwise: Bobby Connell, Bizzy Monte-Sano, Toby Tobin, Ned Hall, Billy Kelly, Vic Romagna, Sam Wakeman, David Elwell, George O'Day, Jory Hinman.

The Crew   3

VIC ROMAGNA: During a long lunch late in '64 Bus asked me what would happen if someone approached him about '67. By the time lunch was over, on the back of an envelope, a crew was formed. That's how it started, and many of those names showed up on *Intrepid*.

As time went on, Bus and I and Buddy Bombard talked a lot about the crew. We sail a lot and while we sail we keep our eyes on certain people. Generally, we find them aboard the boats we are on in races like the Trans-Atlantic and Bermuda. Then we get together and talk. "Gee, so and so is a good one and we ought to keep our eyes on him." The group that had sailed with us on *Weatherly* in '62, of course, provided a great nucleus.

There were a lot of letters. I must have gone through 140 letters from kids stating their qualifications. We knew about most of them before we even got their letters. A letter would come in and we'd say, "Oh, God, he was a troublemaker, or he hasn't got enough experience, or he's the kind of guy that's always sailed a boat but he has never crewed and he'd give us trouble."

BUS MOSBACHER: By the fall of '66 we had a great group of boys who had either called or come to see me. I knew and had sailed with most of

47

them, but if I hadn't sailed with them, maybe Vic had, and if Vic hadn't then there'd be someone we knew darn well and whose opinion we could trust. There were only three or four I hadn't really sailed with even a little bit. And again one of the most important things to us was knowing the boys and knowing they were compatible as well as competent. The perfect combination is a champion small boat sailor who's had a lot of offshore experience and has a high I.Q. and is just a tremendously pleasant and happy guy to have around.

VIC ROMAGNA: We had planned to do some special crew training on *Constellation* when she got back from Europe in the fall of '66, but that didn't work out. We finally decided on the crew and notified them and wrote a letter to the others, saying we had to go with the guys we knew best. Then we sent a questionnaire to the crew asking when they could appear for spring sailing in '67, when they had exams at college, and information like that. We got those back and made a master copy so we knew who would be aboard each boat, each weekend.

We had our first sail on *Connie* on April first. We had lots of people and sort of a general inspection of the boat. The next weekend was about the same with the rest of the group. Some were obvious standouts, others would develop, and a few, who should have been better, were surprising us with ineptness of one sort or another.

We made what I call an organization chart. It was like a station bill [1] and listed the jobs. In other words, there were three guys on the foredeck and certain duties were assigned to them and the same with the halyard man and the winch crankers below deck and the tailers. This was good. You gave a guy his jobs. You impressed upon him that these jobs he must do, that he must do them perfectly, and that he must never turn around to help somebody else because that would leave his job unfinished and that could become more damaging than the one he has gone to help. Of course, when there was some dramatic thing like the time we dumped the spinnaker overboard, there was nothing on the organization chart that would get a spinnaker back on board, so this was an all-hands job. But we talked about this sort of thing constantly and constantly anticipated.

BIZZY MONTE-SANO: Crewing on a 12-Meter is somewhat the opposite of ocean racing. On an ocean racer, each crew member usually takes turns at the various jobs; one fellow will cast off, another will crank, and another tail the line. Then after a while you change so that each guy

[1] Cf. U.S. Navy watch, quarter, and station bill.

does a bit of everything. But on a Twelve everyone sticks to the same job. There is no change. It's just like running a team. In football, where there are set plays, each person has a job to do and he doesn't deviate from it. On *Intrepid,* everyone knew what to do and did it as perfectly as he could. There were very few commands given.

TOBY TOBIN: In '66 I went to Bermuda on a Navy boat and then to Denmark with Jakob Isbrandtsen. My primary contact with *Intrepid* was with Vic Romagna, who sailed regularly with Jakob. I had asked Vic about the possibility of sailing with Bus and he kept his hand pretty close to his chest and said things were very fluid and flexible. When I got back from Denmark, I visited Bus to discuss his plans. Later on, probably in the fall of '66, Bus asked me if I would like to participate. I was able to work it out with the Navy—they officially encourage participation in international competition. We started sailing in April. I was in the process of moving and as my family was in Maryland at the time I spent weekends with Bus. I think he had a pretty good idea then who the crew would be.

VIC ROMAGNA: Bus and I both knew who our best bets were for certain positions and we put them there. Bizzy would be in charge of the foredeck. Bobby Connell would work with Bizzy. We knew Jory Hinman was darn good. He had sailed with Bus on *Easterner* one year and with Bill Cox on *American Eagle.* I've known him all my life. He was quiet, just our type of kid. He never raised his voice, never asked a question, he just put his head down and worked. He worked cleverly and beautifully and we hoped he would be good on the foredeck with Bizzy and Bobby. We needed the calm of Jory up there because Bizzy can get excited at times, although that doesn't effect his capability. We tried other kids up forward but, as anticipated, these three worked beautifully.

BUS MOSBACHER: Bizzy, Bobby, and Jory worked things out themselves in their area. One of the great things was the caliber of all these kids, mentally as well as physically. They knew what they were there for, they had the intelligence and experience to refine what they were doing, and they did it—there were no two ways about it.

As the crew shaped up, and remembering my experience on *Weatherly,* I wanted to be sure we didn't end up with an entire crew the size of Billy Kelly, Buddy Bombard, and Jory Hinman. They just weren't big enough. But we did have room for two or three of them because

On the foredeck, Bizzy Monte-Sano developed a smooth working team with Jory Hinman and Bobby Connell. By mid-season their spinnaker sets and jibes were fast and flawless.

they were good enough and fast enough, as long as we had someone else. So we had a few Neddy Halls and Bobby Connells, who could lay it on thick if we needed them. As it turned out we really didn't need them. Strangely enough, Sam Wakeman and Dave Elwell, who were our grinders, probably weren't the strongest boys we could have had. But they earned their jobs and did well, not so much because of their grinding ability, which was very adequate because the winches were so good, but because of all the other things they could and did do. I never saw two guys work harder. They worked their way onto the boat and they never forgot it. I remember before the last Cup Race, they were down on the boat cleaning their winches and stowing gear and working as hard as they did in June or July when they weren't sure they were going to sail on it.

DAVE ELWELL: At the same time I was trying to get a berth for the Trans-Atlantic Race, I read in *Yachting* that the *Intrepid* Syndicate had been formed. So I wrote Mr. Strawbridge. I said I was going on the Trans-Atlantic Race but for the following summer I was interested in the possibility of sailing on a 12-Meter. I received a reply saying he had my letter and at the appropriate time he would send it to whoever had been selected skipper of the boat. Then I got a letter from Bus asking me to contact him when I returned from Europe. When I got back I went in and spoke with him. At that time he wasn't sure whether he was going to accept the position, but if he did, he said he'd give me an opportunity to try out. He didn't know much about me then and he was as generous as he could have been.

I ended up sailing with them in the spring. I came down just about every weekend from college. I drove from St. Lawrence University in Canton, N.Y., to Syracuse and flew to LaGuardia. It took about four hours and I'd come down Friday night and go back Sunday night. In spite of this, my marks got better because I made myself do a week's work in three days.

For the first couple of weekends, we were split into groups, so the less experienced fellows could work with a couple of older guys. I started out on *Constellation*, cranking a coffee grinder and then they put me tailing one of the winches and I stayed there until the beginning of June. When *Intrepid* was launched, I was given a chance to grind a winch on her.

I guess the first time I was actually asked to sail on the boat was at Yacht Haven marina in Stamford, Conn. Bus asked me, "Would you like to sail on *Intrepid?*" and I said, "Sure, I'd love to." Then I thought it was just for the day or something. Each day I would come down to the dock and *Intrepid* would be on one side and *Constellation* on the other. And I would just kind of stand on the dock waiting, not knowing where to go. I didn't like to hop on *Intrepid* feeling that I was in the boat, because I certainly wasn't. So I'd ask Bus where should I sail, and he'd say on *Intrepid*. Then Bus asked me again if I would like to sail on *Intrepid* and I said sure. Later in the day I began to think about it and said to myself, "Gee, I guess he means this is a somewhat permanent berth." Actually, until the very end, I never felt I had a real position for myself on the boat.

When I first came aboard, I realized what a group this was. They were all older than me, and had all sailed together before. Well, Sam Wakeman hadn't sailed with the other guys, but he'd been on Chandler Hovey's *Easterner,* so he knew more about what was going on than I did. We were the two winch grinders, and were sort of the two bottom men, but I knew enough about the basic operation so that by paying attention I could figure out what I was supposed to do. It was mainly guys like Bizzy and Billy Kelly who gave us tips about specific techniques. I found out the best way to do it was to keep my mouth shut and work out my problems.

TOBY TOBIN: On April 15th all of the eventual first team except George O'Day and Jory Hinman were on board for practice on *Constellation*. The difference from the previous week was marked: it was a great deal more competitive, with more finesse but unfortunately a good bit of noise, too.

There was a very different atmosphere on board this boat compared with that on *Columbia* in the early stages of 1958. Whereas berths on that boat were virtually guaranteed, here there was competition despite the announcement three weeks before that Bus, George, Vic, Bobby, Buddy, Bizzy, Ned, Billy, Jory, Bobby and I were the *Intrepid* crew.

A crew member regretted every mistake: when I missed my footing and fell on a hatch that first day, I felt stupid both because I slipped and because I was afraid of risking my berth.

The weather was nasty—rain, fog, miserable easterly which picked up to over twenty knots by the end of the day. Lying on the weather rail and spattered with salt water, it wasn't long before we abandoned any anti-homosexual scruples and cuddled as closely together as possible for warmth. My hands seemed cold until I gripped the aluminum rollers on the coffee grinder handles, and then they felt like ice.

Connie was more sophisticated than my last 12-Meter—with a bendy mast, bendy boom, two travelers, a rod headstay, stretchluff genoas— but the new boat was to have many more innovations, such as underdeck winch pedestals (the crankers will probably wear miner's helmets) two rudders, a brand new shape and a very interesting deck layout.

Thursday it was tack, double-tack (no triples, thank God) set, jibe, jibe, jibe, luff, off, luff, jibe, luff, off, luff, jibe, douse, tack—three cycles like that. It was a good workout in that wind. By the end of three quick tacks, my arms would keep pumping but nothing happened. The fatigue was not severe, but my muscles were temporarily drained.

BIZZY MONTE-SANO: We began at a high level on *Intrepid*, because almost everyone on board had sailed on Twelves before. I sailed in '62, Bobby Connell sailed in '62 and '64, Buddy Bombard had sailed in '58, '62, and '64, Jory Hinman in '64 and Ned Hall and Billy Kelly sailed in

'62. The only person who had never been on a Twelve was Dave Elwell.

Intrepid was a lot different than *Weatherly* in '62. The deck layout, of course, was new to all of us, so during spring sailing we had to develop new techniques. There were some slight communications difficulties but these were outweighed by the advantages of the layout. In general, the gear was much better.

Because we all felt that Olin's design was better than any other Twelve, that the sails were great, and that as a helmsman and captain, Bus was without equal, each member of the crew wanted to make sure that he was a credit to the operation. I guess I thought I could do a pretty good job because of Bobby Connell and Jory. I had sailed with them for years and had great confidence in them. I knew we worked well together, and that's what you look forward to, working with people that do a good job and blend together.

BOBBY CONNELL: Back in 1962, I was on *Columbia* and Bus, of course, had *Weatherly*. He said then that if he ever did it again, he'd like me to crew for him. So when *Intrepid* got started, Vic mentioned it and Bizzy mentioned it but I don't think Bus said anything for some time. About two months before *Intrepid* was launched, he did talk with me at the New York Yacht Club and discussed what he thought I'd be doing on the boat and asked what I'd like to do. I was sort of hemming and

Mosbacher worked his crew hard. For every maneuver he established a **modus** *operandi that was followed to the letter.*

hawing a little bit, trying not to commit myself, but interested enough to find out if I could get off work or not. If you're in college or the service or you have a contact job in sales, it's easier to get time off. Otherwise, you have to take four months off and there aren't many jobs like that.

Bus talked about putting me on the winches because he thought I was fairly strong. You don't really have to be strong on the winches any more and I just didn't like the idea. Bizzy wanted me on the foredeck with him. That's where I wanted to be, and it worked out that way. I don't think I would have done it if I'd been on the winches.

The boat was laid out a lot differently than other 12-Meters, so nobody knew specifically how things were going to work. We just picked it up as we went along. I think the boat could have been sailed with nine people if they knew what they were doing. It was such an easy boat to sail.

TOBY TOBIN: There was a very special feeling about Newport. As you crossed the Jamestown Bridge the excitement grew and continued to grow without abatement on the ferry ride across the bay. Even crossing in dense fog you knew what was there if you couldn't see it: the gong at Fort Adams, the bell off Goat Island were landmarks you recognized by sound. You knew where Ida Lewis was and Newport Shipyard, Christies and the Moorings and all the other familiar places.

You wondered how many other people had something special to do in Newport. Block Island Week was coming up. The Annapolis–Newport Race had just finished and you smugly doubted if anyone had something as special as your own summer of campaigning a 12-Meter.

Eastbourne Lodge, our house there, was a square-turreted, heavy mansion on Rhode Island Avenue. It was filled with rare stuffed birds that seemed to have escaped from the Smithsonian, but the house retained some of the stately elegance of the era in which it was built, and we looked a little incongruous in sailing clothes in the drawing room.

Bachelor members of the *Intrepid* and *Constellation* crews roomed in group accommodations on the third floor. Senior members of the crew and Olin Stephens lived in quite comfortably furnished quarters, most with private baths and some with sitting rooms.

Our first night we all gathered for an elegant supper with roast beef, champagne, and a birthday cake for Pat Mosbacher. Meals would be civilized—with coat and tie for supper—and satisfying.

And that meal was certainly welcome. The first day's practice after a layoff was a workout. Even the cooling Atlantic southerly couldn't prevent sopping wet shirts and dripping heads as we went through our routine. The jibing drills were much tougher than sail changing and tacking. We did change from three-ounce to five-ounce to nine-ounce jib as the day went on and the five-ounce looked beautiful. We ran out and back along the torpedo range four times—set, jibe, douse, incessantly.

Tacking in a breeze required more sheer power on the grinders than jibing, but jibing involved every man on the boat in a vigorous maneuver, often one that required sustained effort. A long series of them is very wearing, but we needed the drill.

DAVE ELWELL: I gradually got used to grinding the winch down below. The ventilation was not what it could be, but I didn't really think about that much. As far as actually grinding, it was easier because I could get a better footing by standing on the curve of the hull. I could more or less walk up the hull and brace my feet against the ribs. I didn't have to worry about the sheets hitting me in the calves. The only problem was communications. It was hard to get used to for the first month or so. The winches were extremely noisy, which virtually eliminated verbal communication. We could only see the tailers from the waist down and that made hand signals difficult. A lot of times when the tailer wanted to signal both his hands were being used. So we had a combination of hand signals and foot-stomping. We talked about putting a transparent section in the deck so we could see Bizzy, but it wouldn't work because of cleats and winches in the way.

Sometimes I could look up through the hatches and see what was going on, but at the start and rounding marks, when there was a lot of excitement, I just had to imagine what was happening. I could do that, and I think that's why I got the job over some of the heftier guys.

We gradually oriented ourselves, Sam and I, to what was going on, and by the end of summer, communications were virtually eliminated except for "Start" and "Stop." We had it figured out how fast we were to go at certain times. We could feel the level of the boat. We could see the horizon aft so we got an idea of how the boat was heeling. And we knew if it was blowing only five knots, we took the cranking very easy. Each day, after the first couple of tacks it became more or less automatic. We got the feel of the tacks and how fast Bus was bringing the boat around, how hard it was blowing, when we should start cranking, and how hard it should be, and when we were coming close to the end of the trim.

We realized when an operation was about to begin. Then Bus would say "Ready about," and actually it would be another ten or fifteen seconds before we went to work. So we would just get ready on our winches. We could definitely feel when the jib had been released and the boat started coming around. Sometimes we would get a signal from the guy on the tacking line [2] when the clew of the jib was clear of the mast so that we could start trimming. Just feeling the boat come level, we knew the clew could clear the mast or was close to it and we would start cranking. If we were too soon, the tailer just wouldn't take it in. We could tell by looking at the tailer's legs if he was taking in. We could also feel through our winch handle if the tailer had a strain on the sheet. Even if there was a strain and the tailer was not taking it in, we could feel it.

With a ten-second set on a spinnaker, the timing was very fine. When the time came to crank, we really cranked as hard as we could go. The combination of noise and the fact that we weren't looking at the tailer made it hard to coordinate operations.

I remember once when I was cranking Billy Kelly's drum, he was supposed to ease the spinnaker sheet and pick up the after guy. The after guy and jib sheet were lying side by side at his ankle and Billy picked up the jib sheet. I started to crank when I was supposed to and I realized there should have been more pressure on the line, but I was supposed to be cranking and before Billy realized what was going on, we pulled the jib sheet right through the block.

BIZZY MONTE-SANO: Before we got to a windward mark, I'd ask the navigator what the apparent wind would be for the leeward leg. That affected our choice of spinnaker and also told us how to trim. After discussing it with Bobby and Jory, I'd tell Bus what spinnaker we thought we should use and he'd say, "Okay, Bizzy," or sometimes, "Well, I think we'd do better with the three-quarter-ounce."

Up forward, we decided what the right position of the pole would be. We'd try to get it level at what we thought the correct height for the day would be. Then Bobby or Jory or I would look and say, we're so far from the mark, so we'd get ready to hoist the spinnaker. We decided when it should go up. We tried doing it on command from Bus but that wasn't necessary and at the mark Bus had a lot of other things on his mind. So we decided when to hoist. We usually couldn't see the mark but we could feel the bow start to swing and when we felt we were around the mark, we'd go.

[2] Line used to pull genoa jib forward and around the mast when tacking.

Eastbourne Lodge at Newport provided pleasant headquarters for the men who sailed Intrepid *and* Constellation. *Mosbacher sat at the head of the table, flanked by Olin Stephens and some senior crew members. Breakfast was at seven thirty a.m., dinner from seven to nine thirty p.m., depending on the wind.*

I guess some of the spinnaker sets that looked the best were when we just bore off around the mark and pulled up the spinnaker. I don't think we felt these were our best. The jibe set, when we rounded the mark, jibed, and set the spinnaker on the other side, took longer but was one of our better maneuvers, at least relative to the way it was done by other people.

It didn't matter how far back the other boat was. On *Intrepid,* we always tried to get the spinnaker up as quickly as we could. It was a race within a race and we wanted to handle ours more sharply and more crisply than the other boat.

There were a lot of new ideas on *Intrepid,* but when it came to jibing the spinnaker, we went back to the *Vim* jibe system developed in 1958. We modified it to suit our layout, but there were no basic changes in the system.

We had little things we developed, like an endless line that went around the headstay, so we could take the spinnaker halyard around to the leeward side without having to go up on the bow, which would disturb the skipper and make the boat pound more. He could feel it and probably even tell you who it was with his eyes shut.

In '62 we put our spinnaker on deck in a turtle, but in '67 it was kept below in a bin and came right up from there. Once during the trials we hooked the sheets onto one spinnaker, and the halyard onto the head of another spinnaker which had fallen down from the bin above. When we hauled that sail up, there was nothing attached to the clews. The other sail was pulled up by the after guy. So we sort of had two spinnakers up. The sails were all the same color so it was an easy mistake to make, but I guess from the crewing standpoint that was a low point. Everybody was pretty gloomy. On the second time around, coming upwind, Bus said, "What spinnaker do you think we ought to put up this time?" and I said, "I don't know, Bus, why don't we put them all up and let you take your choice?" Well, that broke the ice. The only reason I said it was because we were leading quite comfortably and I thought everybody's spirits needed a little lifting and an offhand remark might help.

Communication with winch grinders below wasn't always easy. Here, Elwell (left) and Sam Wakeman get a hand signal from the tailer standing on the platform at right.

With the winches linked together and four men grinding, **Intrepid** *had more power and speed than she needed for trimming the genoa in a tacking duel. Low gear was never used.*

BUS MOSBACHER: Jory Hinman was the one who hooked up the spinnakers and he was as completely upset as anyone you've ever seen. He was practically in tears. It was a perfectly understandable mistake. There were a couple of sails in each bin below, and I grant you they were supposed to have had their three corners tied together to prevent this. But one of them had just been up, so they weren't. After setting two spinnakers Jory felt God-awful about it. Then a little later we had Bizzy's classic remark and everybody had a laugh and I think even poor Jory felt better.

TOBY TOBIN: I started out as sort of a utility man up around the mast, working on halyards and gathering the spinnaker on take-downs. One morning up in Newport when I came aboard Vic said, "Toby, you're navigating today." So I became navigator. We had simple but very effective equipment. There was a Swedish plotting gimmick that Olin gave us. Since you can't use the Decca system on the Twelves, navigation was a question of keeping an accurate dead-reckoning position and

TOBY
TOBIN

maintaining it meticulously. It was a mechanical function.

I kept a plot which was oriented to the layline and it was my job to say to Bus, "You are going to be on the layline in a minute and a half and after you get there it will be seven and a half minutes to fetch the mark." This data obviously was revised because of wind and current shifts. The current on the Cup course wasn't predictable. I couldn't tell much on the first windward leg, but the second time to weather, if I could see that the mark tug was lying the way it was the first time, I could crank in the experience I had on the first leg.

There wasn't much about the current in any books. There is a diagram in Eldridge's,[3] but it was pretty hard to check in any detail for that area. I spent some time with the fishermen, who were extremely helpful about currents along the shore. I tried hard during the August series to get the marker tugs to do some experiments for me. I wanted them to stream a drogue[4] and record current direction and velocity every hour they were anchored on the Cup course. The Race Committee thought that would be giving us unfair advantage and they would not let the tugs do it. Before a start, I used to throw over a folded newspaper and check its drift against the Cup buoy. That gave us a vague idea of the current at the moment.

We had very accurate odometers from Kenyon Marine, which gave us the distance run. Direction was taken from the helmsman's compass. Another aid that made it pretty easy to keep track of the shifting laylines were some plastic triangles. We had an eighty, a seventy, and a sixty-five-degree triangle which I used in plotting the laylines and what we'd be doing on the next tack. I got so I could tell pretty clearly whether we were going to tack in sixty-eight or seventy-two degrees. That was a matter of experience, getting to know the boat and what she would do under different conditions.

As navigator I was also responsible for weather information. We tried to get as much dope as we could. I'd listen to the Boston marine operator first thing in the morning and I'd call up the ESSA[5] station. I also had a contact at the Naval Air Station. The Race Committee gave out a forecast prepared for them by the U.S. Weather Bureau in Boston. My friends at the Navy Base copied this and would tell me what the Race Committee report was going to be, then tell me whether they thought it was any good. We also listened to the FAA broadcast on the beacon band, which gave actual reports of weather at different airports. If there was a front moving in, I could usually tell about where it was by listening to what was going on at the different places. I also listened

60

[3] Tide and current tables.
[4] A sea anchor.
[5] Environmental Science Services Administration.

to the fishermen when it was foggy to hear what they said about visibility. I think we covered most of the available sources before we left the dock. All this had some bearing on our choice of sails, and also provided Bus with basic information.

We didn't do much racing when we had thick fog; the Committee usually canceled. But our practice was not curtailed by fog. I can remember being frightened to death sailing around in Narragansett Bay. We had a little course there which was a good drill. It was about 750 yards long, just to the west of Rose Island. We completed this course in a matter of minutes. I can remember lots of days when I had to time our approach to the leeward mark. It took us about fifteen seconds to get the spinnaker down and I had to tell the guys to take it down before I could see the mark. It was that thick. It was pretty scary. There were some times when I could barely see the bow of the boat. Nothing happened, but it could have. *Dame Pattie* went on the rocks at one point during the summer.

I was exaggerating when I said I was scared. I meant I was concerned

During the infrequent breathing spells, the crew stopped sails and stowed them.

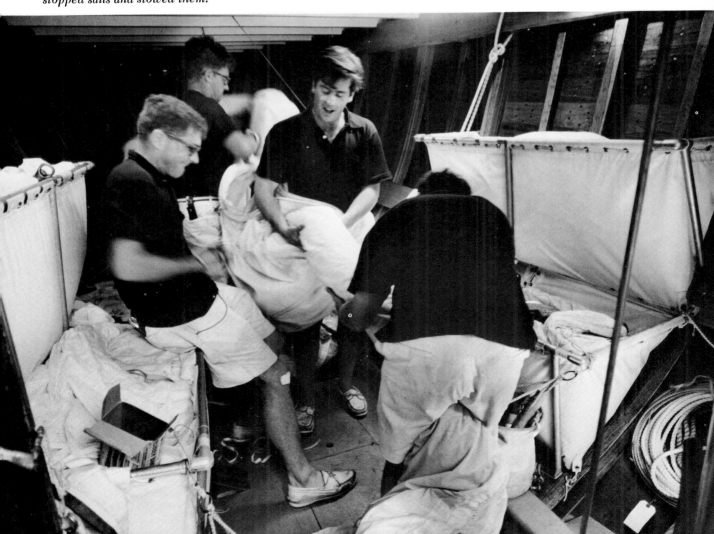

TOBY
TOBIN and I thought the risk probably wasn't worth the training we were deriving from it. A serious crash could have set us back days, maybe weeks, for repairs to the boat. As it turned out, I was wrong. We practiced maybe twenty or thirty days in extraordinarily thick fog and never had an accident. To have missed that training all summer would probably have affected the performance of the group.

Bus was an extremely fierce competitor and was reluctant to miss any opportunity for training. I suppose I should have been flattered that he trusted me to keep us out of trouble—I *was* flattered by it, but I was very tired at the end of one of those days. It wasn't physical exhaustion but just being under pressure all day long.

I made a couple of mistakes during the summer. Fortunately neither one cost us anything, but Bus rightly insisted on having everything perfect. He expected me to perform at the same level of expertise that he performed at himself. If you didn't meet these standards, he could be sharp, but I wouldn't want to sail with anyone in a Cup Race who didn't demand a high level of performance.

BOBBY CONNELL: One thing the crew realized—Bus knew each man's job as well as he knew it and if you made a mistake, he spotted it. You didn't have to turn around and look at him, because you realized he was aware of it. So you tried to do everything right the first time. I remember one day when I didn't. Bus was a little irritable about his cockpit crew because they were messing up a bit. When the spinnaker came down my job was to take out the main outhaul and I forgot. I tried

Tobin kept a very accurate dead-reckon-track of Intrepid's *course on his plotting board (left). Squares represent nautical miles. Graph with series of curves, developed by Stephens, was used to determine what the apparent wind would be on the reaching legs.*

Mosbacher checked boat speed with the dual indicators on the forward bulkhead of the cockpit. Below these was wind direction indicator. With grease-pencil notes on a piece of plastic, the navigator gives the helmsman course, current data, time to layline.

taking it out when we were on the wind and broke it. Bus got very upset. It was one of the few times I'd heard him get excited. He thought someone from the cockpit had given the order to take the outhaul out and he came out with something like, "Goddammit, who told you to do it?" And I said, "Goddammit, I just *did* it." And that was the end of it.

DAVE ELWELL: I was very much concerned the day I got seasick. I felt that Bus had every right in the world to bring on somebody else, because when it got rough he could hardly tolerate somebody who was going to conk out. That was when he needed them most. But it was a rough day out, it was hot and we'd been working and I did get sick. At

63

the time it was kind of laughed off and then Bus spoke to me afterwards. He asked, "What about this seasickness?" He wasn't trying to rub it in. He was just trying to find out where I stood.

I told him I had been seasick on occasion but sometimes it could be blowing twice as hard as that day and it wouldn't bother me at all. Bus asked me if I'd taken pills and I hadn't. He suggested that I buy some and see if they would help. I took the pills and I don't think they helped me at all, but I didn't get seasick anymore.

BOBBY CONNELL: Dave was a sweet little college kid in the beginning. Then he started loosening up and everybody came to know him a bit and he turned out to be a dirty rotten guy like the rest of us by the end of the season. He won the award one day for being the only one on *Intrepid* to get seasick. We had a couple of vulnerable people. Bus himself was susceptible and Bizzy was another booter, as we called it. Billy Kelly turned green once in a while but he didn't become actively sick. David was such a meek and mild person he asked Bus's permission to use the leeward rail to get sick, which I thought was kinda nice.

BIZZY MONTE-SANO: In 1962 on *Weatherly* we made a practice of giving "awards," and we resurrected this in '67. An award was given for the biggest goof of the day. It was an orange sweat shirt, and we passed it around on the boat to whoever won it.

When we started the award, Bobby Connell and I thought very seriously about it. We said to ourselves, was there anybody on the boat we could give it to who would take offense? And when we answered that question in the negative, it seemed all right.

It was a real tribute to the group that we could give an award to a fellow who had made a mistake in such a way that he didn't really feel bad about it. We were able to laugh at ourselves and our mistakes because each one knew that the others never doubted his ability. Everyone knew the guy getting the award was really doing his job. To me this signified the great understanding and cohesiveness of the group.

I remember the day we had two spinnakers up and somebody asked if Jory was going to get the orange sweat shirt. David Elwell, who was an absolute delight, said, "Hell no, he's going to get a whole orange suit and sneakers to match." So while we were dead earnest about sailing, we had some laughs.

VIC ROMAGNA: Bizzy was another Bob Hope, a natural comedian. We had a number of them on board, but he was by far the best. Nothing

64

As navigator, Tobin monitored weather broadcasts and listened to transmissions from fishermen.

stereotype, no clichés, just spur-of-the-moment humor. It just fractured us and was a great antidote for tension.

BUS MOSBACHER: I was very much against picking on anybody who had made a mistake. I wouldn't want to berate him or embarrass him because everybody on the boat knew who had made a mistake. I gave him the opportunity to do it over again and he almost always got it right the second time. If he didn't get it by the third or fourth time he was not the right man for the particular job. I certainly asked a lot of the crew and we went out and practiced until most of them were just about ready to drop. I thought they'd had a full day, but by the time we'd get back to the dock and maybe have a Coke or a beer, most of them went swimming or surfing or played football, so there was still some energy left.

They knew what they were there for. They volunteered for this job and they had a great interest in it and pride in doing it well. Some of those days were awfully long. My own feeling was that it became fairly obvious when you got to the point where someone was at the end of his physical ability. But we never pushed anyone beyond where he was willing to go.

GEORGE O'DAY: I've watched Bus sailing for I don't know how many miles, and he knows exactly when to tack and when not to tack. He did it with *Weatherly* in '62 and he got this skill only by going out and practicing. He would drive the crew crazy, but if you're a helmsman, you have to do it this way. Nothing else works—you just have to practice thousands of times.

BIZZY MONTE-SANO: During the summer we had one serious overriding turn on the winch. We were coming up to the finish line and had to make one more tack. I remember we decided to cut the wire sheet because it was the only way to free it to tack. I went and got the wire cutters and Bobby and I cut it just as we tacked and the genoa was trimmed with the other sheet. I remember cutting it close to the clew so there wouldn't be any wire slapping around.

Another day we broke a light messenger used to take the spinnaker halyards aloft. This was one of the little things we did to save weight and reduce windage aloft. So we pulled Jory Hinman up the mast to reeve a new messenger. Then we set the floater—the light, half-ounce spinnaker. Jory was up the mast when we rounded the mark about a minute ahead of *Columbia,* and we ended up twenty minutes ahead of them, so we talked about keeping Jory up the mast all the time to make us go faster. Aside from these incidents, we had few problems.

On *Weatherly* in '62 we broke quite a few spinnaker guys, but in '67 we had new procedures and used a reaching strut which reduced the strain on the guy by about forty per cent. When you had the spinnaker pole against the headstay, the pole and the guy tended to line up. So when you trimmed the guy, it resulted in tremendous compression on the pole. By putting a reaching strut out from the mast you changed the angle of pull and reduced the compression and strain. It also kept the guy off the titanium shrouds, which were supposedly weakened by abrasions.

DAVE ELWELL: By the end of the summer, I could have held my own with anybody grinding winches. But in the beginning I was skeptical about my ability. Had the winches been on deck so Bus could have seen the effort I had to put out to get results, he might have thought twice about keeping me aboard.

As time went on, I thought the whole crew developed an unusual spirit. Everybody had one main interest, and that was sailing. Everyone wanted to do the best job possible, not because they were representing the country or the Yacht Club, we felt we were representing *Intrepid* as a group and ourselves as individuals.

TOBY TOBIN: Bus was a demanding skipper but there were no written or stated rules about personal behavior. Bus never said, "Go to bed at ten o'clock." We had no conditioning program, but at least half the crew did some form of exercise to keep in shape. There were no rules about drinking. Cocktails were always available at Eastbourne every night. Very few of us had more than one and a great many had soft drinks. Bus expected people to behave maturely and responsibly. However, he did have a mysterious antenna system which somehow let him know when someone was staying up late and the next day that guy would find himself pretty busy on board.

VIC ROMAGNA: Bobby Connell would find himself a girl and go out for the evening and come back rather late. We would know it and the next day in practice we would throw everything we could at Bobby to try to make him foul up. During the day, having had a little less sleep and a little more to drink, he would have to work twice as hard to make sure he didn't foul up and make a mistake, but he was letter-perfect.

On many occasions when Neddy Hall looked a little tired, we would do a lot of jibing to the port side, trying to foul him up. It was only when you could make him foul up that you could say later, "Neddy, you shouldn't have gone out and did you find what you were after last night?" But then when we weren't able to foul them up, they'd turn around with big smiles on their faces, knowing very well what we were doing.

BUS MOSBACHER: There were funny stories about waking up in the middle of the night and hearing people on the gravel driveway that ran from the parking lot to the house. Fortunately I used to sleep like a log, especially when we had long days—and they really were long days out on that boat, and at my age they were tiring. After a nice hot shower, a cold drink, and a good dinner, I was ready to sleep.

One night for some reason I got up, had a drink of water, and just as I was going back into bed, I heard footsteps on that gravel driveway. I walked over to the window. There was Neddy Hall running in from the parking space, along the lawn, then two steps on the gravel to get around the edge of the hedge, and back on the lawn again. I wasn't going to say much about it. It wasn't a night before a race, but just before the trials when we were sailing hard every day. I was on my way back to bed, or even already in bed when damned if I didn't hear a car come in again. I went to the window and who was it but Dave Rockefeller. So the next day I didn't say a word. I told Pat about it and said,

"Don't say anything, they're doing a good job, what the heck."

That day we were out sailing and I heard this horrendous explosion. It was Neddy, and when he wants to cuss, he can cuss. Neddy just exploded, you know, blah, blah, blah. After it all calmed down, Vic or somebody said, "What in the world happened to Neddy?" Well, apparently he had been up forward and had come up under one of those winches on the mast. He must have cracked his head real hard and was entitled to cuss.

That evening after our showers we were all down at the little bar in the living room pouring a drink. Neddy came over to get himself a beer and I looked at him and said, "Neddy, how's your head?"—meaning, how's your head from the crack on the winch. He just looked at me and said, "Goddammit, I don't know how you knew, but I knew you'd know. Don't you ever sleep?" I started to laugh and said, "I meant when you banged your head on the winch." "Oh," he said. "But," I said, "I do think you were up a little late and I certainly hope it was worthwhile." He said, "No, Goddammit, it wasn't even worthwhile." Every-

The crew responded instinctively to critical situations. When they got an overriding turn in the genoa sheet, an auxiliary sheet was quickly rigged to the backstay winch. Wirecutters freed the fouled sheet and the boat was ready to tack within a few seconds.

body heard about this and Neddy admitted he got caught coming in late. Everybody needled him for a couple of weeks.

A while later Pat and I went down and spent the night with Mr. and Mrs. Seymour St. John—he's the headmaster at Choate. We came in the next morning and both crews were sitting in the foyer reading newspapers and waiting for the lunches to be carried to the cars. They all stood up and cheered and said, "A new record had been set, the old record by Neddy was broken. Bus has it now." And who was the cheerleader in this needling but David Rockefeller. So I said, "You know, David, Neddy really didn't have the record at all." "What do you mean?" he said. "Well," I said, "the same night Neddy came in at a quarter to three, you came in at three-fifteen." David said incredulously, "You knew, of course. And that was the only time I was out all summer."

BIZZY MONTE-SANO: I think anyone who felt like it could have stayed out all night, but Bus picked people who weren't likely to do that. He picked people who fundamentally liked to sail, wanted to race, and wanted to do this in the best way possible. If you have people like that you don't have to tell them what time to be in. They realized that as members of the crew Bus was depending on them.

We used to joke about the crew getting together to have the driveway paved because they always knew Bus and Pat could hear whoever came in late at night.

HAROLD VANDERBILT: Comparing amateur and professional crews, I'd say they were equally good, but both require a great deal of organization and intensive practice.

WILLIE CARSTENS: The boys on *Intrepid* were good, really good, because they were doing something they liked and they did it the best way possible. Now, the crew on *Ranger*, when I was mate for Mr. Vanderbilt, was all paid, but they took pride in their job too. It was an honor to be on a boat like that. Both those crews had great spirit, and that's because Mr. Vanderbilt and Mr. Mosbacher were so much alike.

GEORGE O'DAY: If I was asked tomorrow to sail a 12-Meter, I wouldn't do it if Bus was sailing another. I'd prefer to put my career aside and sail with this guy because I enjoy it so much. He's got a little bit of something I don't have. He could get that crew that I loved to work with—it was a perfectionist team.

New York Yacht Club Race Committee—1967: (left to right) Charles Morgan, Peter Geddes, Nicholas Potter, Robert H. Wessmann, Willis M. Fanning, Chairman Henry H. Anderson, Jr., B. Devereux Barker, III, and William Burnham, conducted the Trial Races and America's Cup Races.

Racing

4

TOBY TOBIN: On Friday April 28th *Intrepid* was launched amid the cheers of about six hundred people. The day was cold but bright and after Straw said, "Time and tide wait for no man," Mrs. Bartram broke the champagne bottle on the second try. *Intrepid* went down (vertically on an elevator) and floated exactly on her lines.

The jam to see her was heavy and very nearly sank the float to which she was moored after launching. On deck two oil drums were covered with canvas to simulate big winches, although most people knew the real coffee grinders would be below decks.

The boat had many remarkable features. She surely had the highest ballast-displacement ratio of any Twelve—nearly seventy per cent. There were fantastic new savings in weight. She had few winches on deck. The boom was only 150 pounds and very close to the deck. To save weight, there was no clew outhaul fitting: a tail led around a block on the boom end to the outhaul pendant.

Her strange underbody, cutaway deadwood, and twin rudders were obviously departures. She tested as well as *Constellation* in every way and better in many. She was short overall with a pronounced knuckle at the bow. From aft, she looked like a whole boat set on a fin keel.

Her sophistication was marvelous. The top of the spar was titanium, as was all the rigging. The bar rigging, made of solid strips instead of wire, even had titanium rollers. The tangs were internal. There was a strain gauge mounted on the headstay and on each backstay. They worked electrically by measuring the expansion of the tangs when under load and gave a reading in pounds on a dial in the cockpit.

The wheel was a space-age marvel, with wheels, clutches, and brakes. The two rudders could be independent or linked in line or at any differential. The plan was to use the trim tab at about four degrees to give lift to the keel and neutralize the main steering rudder. She was quite a boat.

BUS MOSBACHER: We were happy with *Intrepid* right from the beginning. The first day was very light and she didn't go too well against *Constellation*. But we felt she was about the same as *Connie* and that was good. All the design ideas that went into *Intrepid* would help her out in rough water—things like shortening her ends and taking the weight out of them. So we were a little anxious but not disappointed when we didn't do so well in the smooth water on the Sound. Olin had said we were going to have to work hard in light weather, but when it blew, there would be no holding her.

OLIN STEPHENS: As a design, *Intrepid* was distinctly better than *Constellation* before *Constellation* was changed. *Intrepid* had a wider range of speed, she could point equally as high as *Connie* and foot considerably faster when she was rapped off a little bit. However, after the addition of the kicker on *Constellation*—one had already been added to *Columbia*—*Intrepid* didn't have such an advantage over these boats.

TOBY TOBIN: In practice-sailing it appeared that *Intrepid* was a very fast boat—and the more wind, the faster she was. The tab rudder made a noticeable difference. We climbed to windward very quickly on *Constellation*. Olin told Bus not to worry about starts, just get free air. I hoped his confidence was justified. It was most impressive in a man as cautious and withdrawn as he.

BILL STRAWBRIDGE: Bus had his training program all worked out. He knew just how far each day he was going with the crew in practicing certain things. He had it timed so that at the end he had brought them up to a pitch of excellence—they had every maneuver they wanted to make down to perfection.

TOBY TOBIN: Before the start of the New York Yacht Club's Spring

Regatta, we went through two cycles of practice: tacking, setting, jibing, and dousing. The wind that day was southeast six to ten knots.

The course for the race was windward, leeward, windward. At the start we hit the line a boat length to leeward of *Constellation*, ahead of *Weatherly* by four lengths and to weather and ahead of *American Eagle*. The boat delighted us by leaping ahead almost immediately. It was a very satisfying way to start our first race, which had us all pretty excited in spite of our successful trials with *Connie*.

In the New York Yacht Club's Spring Regatta, Constellation *leads* American Eagle *and* Weatherly *in close quarters as the boats square away for the downwind leg.* Intrepid *had already rounded.*

Intrepid was vulnerable going downwind in light air. In this race on the Sound in June, American Eagle slides by her with apparent ease. Mosbacher shifted to a smaller spinnaker and held his own. On the windward leg to the finish Intrepid took the lead and won by a minute.

TOBY
TOBIN

At the weather mark we were two minutes ahead of *Constellation*, which was about a half a minute ahead of *Eagle*. We set a Hood three-quarter-ounce, fifty-foot chute which seemed much too deep. *Eagle* gained alarmingly and finally passed us. After we changed to a three-quarter-ounce, forty-five-foot spinnaker, we began to pick up on *Eagle* throughout the jibing duel all the way down the rest of the leg. Bus worked the angles beautifully, frequently caught *Eagle* off guard and came up to the mark in position to starboard tack her. Whether because she had just jibed and felt she couldn't jibe back, or because they thought they could make it across our bow, they fouled us. Bus had to swing sharply to miss them and Commodore Pratt on *Eagle* at least registered some facial concern at the situation. Surprisingly, after what seemed to us a clear foul, *Eagle* did not withdraw at that time.

We rounded a length behind her with a beautiful douse and then we tacked twice and had *Eagle* under control. We pulled ahead steadily and led by a minute at the finish. *Intrepid's* windward performance was great but spinnaker choice was really critical.

BUS MOSBACHER: Sailing *Intrepid,* as with any boat, was a matter of balance. This involved everything from hull design to sails and distribution of crew. But to relate it directly to steering—if all the other factors have been worked out—you have a finely tuned machine that should be kept balanced. This balance, once you have found the right combination of wind and trim, is usually transmitted reasonably well through the feeling of pressure on the helm. This was not constant and would vary in different weights of wind and different sea conditions. But as you get to know your boat, you have a feeling for when she is going her optimum speed. You have to know your boat, and that takes many hours of practice.

Mosbacher sailed every race as though his life depended on it. His reflexes were completely attuned to the motion of the hull, the flow of wind on his face, the pressure he felt on the wheel.

Racing takes complete concentration. This is why you often see somebody steering a boat in peculiar positions with a peculiar look on his face. The boys have always kidded me about wagging my head. I was never conscious of this until they told me about it. But it's all part of concentration, sensing the angle of heel you are trying to maintain, watching the seas as they approach, feeling the increase or decrease in wind on your face. You must become a part of the boat, or it must become an extension of you.

You can't think about sailing these boats in close quarters if you have to stop and worry about how far the bow is away from you. You've got to be able to look at a hole and drive through it or decide you can't get through just as you do with your car. When you're driving, you don't turn the wheel X number of degrees to get around a corner. You turn automatically—the car is an extension of you going around the corner.

As time went on I got the rhythm of *Intrepid* and steering her became a spontaneous reaction.

TOBY TOBIN: We came up to the last race in the observation trials on the Sound with a record of six wins and one loss. *American Eagle* had the same record, but the only race we lost was to her when *Intrepid* made a mistake in navigation. We rounded the wrong mark on a leeward leg and had to go back and "unwind" our string from the buoy. In the process *Eagle* went by and we lost three minutes. We made a good recovery but couldn't catch her.

But in the final race of this series we really trounced *Eagle*. We sailed a twenty-mile windward-leeward-windward course in an eight-to-ten knot southwester. We built up a big lead going to weather, gained some off the wind and won by five and a half minutes. We had two errors in the race. We lost the spinnaker toppinglift and solved this by using the spare spinnaker halyard as a lift. Then on the final leg, we had an overiding turn on the next to last tack which forced us to cut the genoa sheet. The sheets were greasy and Buddy Bombard had to take four turns to hold the strain and that caused the snarl. We rigged a spare sheet, cut the fouled one and tacked for the finish.

Our plan to get a final weekend's practice in Long Island Sound was aborted when the mast broke Saturday afternoon, June twentieth, about 4 p.m., under no particular strain, sailing to weather in about fifteen knots of wind. We were not sure what the failure was—the starboard main spreader or the internal starboard tang.

TOBY
TOBIN

When the spar went, there was a loud crack below, louder and more ominous than those we'd heard as the chain plates and tie rods worked slightly under heavy load. Almost immediately the boat began to straighten up and most of us guessed what had happened.

But one of the pleasures of sailing with a crew like this is their ability to respond to a new situation without hesitation, confusion, or shouting. Bus said later he was puzzled as to what he should do. There ought to be an order for such situations, but it wasn't necessary, as the crew did what could be done spontaneously.

With a loud crack, Intrepid's *mast snapped while she was sailing to windward on the Sound in a fifteen-knot breeze. The break, which was not complete, occurred right at the lower spreaders and the bar rigging came down in a menacing tangle.*

The fractured spar hung overside, held by the internal halyards. The remaining mast stump was supported by the lower shrouds.

Right: The crew went forward, cut the jib halyard and secured the genoa. The top of the broken spar was pulled aboard toward the port quarter by taking up on the backstay.

Below: Intrepid's well organized list of crew assignments hadn't made provision for broken mast drill but every man quickly found a job and did it as though it was routine.

Above: The broken end of the mast was held to the stump by a tongue of metal. After this gave way, it was possible to lower away on the internal halyards and control the broken section.

Getting the mainsail off was a problem. A man was hoisted to the top of the stump by the spinnaker pole lift. He passed a bight inside luff so sail could be winched down.

When a mast goes, it is difficult to determine what part or fitting went first. In this case, an internal titanium tang was blamed. Later the verdict changed to spreader failure.

We got the upper end of the spar aboard by heaving around on the backstay and the gantline. The jib halyard was cut and the sail taken off and the problem of getting the main under control was isolated. We took it off the boom, for reasons not clear to me, after which it flailed menacingly, uncontrolled from luff to leach, scything the air with the heavy wire, outhaul pendant.

We found that the combined strength of the crew was not enough to subdue the sail by brute force and several lines passed around it were only partially effective because they were not high enough. We sent a man to the top of the stump by elevating him on the spinnaker pole chain. He passed a bight of line inside the luff and we managed to winch the sail down off the damaged track.

The upper section of the mast was gradually working at the break and it was clear that metal fatigue would sever the two pieces. Most of us expected a violent crash when they separated, forgetting that the internal halyards would hold the upper section up. As soon as it parted, this became obvious and we merely lowered away to let the section settle enough to get the upper end clear of the water and to make it possible to lash the other end to the stump.

Once secure, we towed back to City Island in a mood of subdued jocularity. We were relieved that no one was hurt, concerned by the delay and expense of the repair, puzzled about the cause of the failure. All of us felt, curiously, that we ought to be jovial to keep up morale and yet remained conscious of the importance of not giving offense by light-heartedness in a serious situation.

The boat was cleaned up and the crew secured at 8 p.m. Shortly thereafter, the other mast was stepped and we towed to Newport only two days behind schedule.

Once in Newport, we drilled constantly. The general pattern was to circle endlessly around two buoys about three quarters of a mile apart, making sail changes every few minutes. Practicing against *Constellation,* we found she was much faster with the kicker added. The purpose of this skeg is to reduce the quarter wave, which it obviously does, and this adds a bit to boat speed.

Columbia was also hard at work. She was a different boat from the one I remembered in 1958. Among major changes, she was very clean on deck and this impression was accentuated by her flush hatches. Her boom was low and appeared even lower because of the crown on her deck, and the pedestals on her coffee grinders were cut down. She had had a kicker put on some time before, and we all wondered how that would affect her speed.

BIZZY MONTE-SANO: We had raced against *American Eagle* and had practiced with *Constellation* since early spring, but we didn't know about *Columbia.* I began to worry about her and I guess everyone else did, too.

BUS MOSBACHER: By the time we got to Newport, I thought I had a fairly good idea of how *Intrepid* would go in different wind conditions. She seemed somewhat faster than *Constellation* and *Eagle* going to windward but both these boats were as good, if not better, reaching and running. This was especially true in wind ranges of four to six knots. When the breeze got up to ten knots *Intrepid's* performance improved considerably.

Because we had what appeared to be the faster boat upwind, it became definite policy not to mix with anyone at the start. Our whole theory was to get on the starting line with clear wind and let her go. This doesn't do your ego any good. It's much nicer to get in there and mix it up and maybe once in a while win a few starts. That's good for everyone's enthusiasm on the boat. But it's not smart if you have a faster boat. The quickest way to lose with *Intrepid* was to foul out. If you have a slower boat, you have to do it with mirrors and take all sorts of chances. We did that with *Vim* against *Columbia* in the 1958 trials and were within inches of fouling all the time. We never did, but our tactics then were quite different. We got into that tail-chasing business. You try to get on a fellow's tail going away from the line—preferably on starboard tack—then as he starts to jibe you swing off and he can't jibe in front of you. If he starts to tack, you luff up inside him and he can't tack into you, so you just herd him away from the line indefinitely. There are only two boats in the race so it doesn't make any difference when you get back to the line as long as you make your move properly and get there before he does. But in '67, with one or two exceptions, our starts were defensive rather than offensive as they were on *Vim*. I tried to start *Intrepid* to windward of the competition and keep out of trouble. Consequently most of our starts were pretty dull for the spectators.

TOBY TOBIN: On the starts I was responsible for keeping time, reporting the course to the first mark, reckoning the current, and looking for wind shifts. As a rule we didn't do any time-run on the line. Bus kind of did it by feel while he sparred with his opponent. i would report the bearing of the buoy or committee boat, whichever was appropriate, and then our relative position to the starting line. Then, I was also responsible for checking to see if there was a recall signal. Funny thing about checking the current: we used to surreptitiously drop a wad of newspaper over by the Cup buoy and watch what happened to it, but *Columbia* made no bones about it. They came out and dropped a tall buoy and checked that.

BUS MOSBACHER: Going upwind after a start, Toby kept a plotting board so that at any given instant he could tell me, "We have two minutes (or five minutes) to the layline on this tack." He watched his compass very carefully for lifts and headers and he would immediately amend his plot and the calculated time to the layline. It was all done in distance on the plotting board but I asked him to give it to me in time and he did this almost instantaneously. He, of course, had the time to the layline on either tack and also the distance and time to the windward mark. This gave the boys an opportunity to set up for the reach and get their spinnaker gear ready. Actually, this was ready almost all the time and all they needed was the decision as to which spinnaker to use. We usually left that until we were within two to four minutes of the mark.

Intrepid started to reach her outstanding capability when the wind got up to ten knots. Under that it was a little more difficult. But at ten and over she definitely came alive. Her speed went up sharply. Somewhere in the $6\frac{1}{2}$- to seven-knot range her speed relative to other boats improved rapidly and she felt great.

I didn't sail her by any one thing, like the luff of the sail. I looked at the sails, the water, and the wind direction. Obviously, I checked the speedometer, especially in light weather, because you can fool yourself very quickly. The speedometers we had were excellent and they were tremendously helpful in making sure we weren't doing something silly. We knew how fast we should be going in a given amount of breeze, and we knew if we should be going seven and were only doing six, we'd better do something. But I would say the speedometer was a check rather than a primary indicator of how the boat was being sailed.

The wind indicator was something I used for the first time in '67. I found it tremendously valuable—not so much more valuable than a plain old piece of wool in the rigging, but *Intrepid's* boom was so low you couldn't see the weather shrouds if you were sitting to leeward. You couldn't see the masthead fly from there either. In fact, I could only observe the jib about up to the mitre.

I also found the compass, like the speedometer, was important to check on. First and most important, it helps you spot wind shifts so you know when you are being headed or lifted. This isn't quite so important if you are ahead because then you have to do what your opponent is doing. It's more important if you're behind: you can tack when you're headed or make him tack when he's lifted. You gain a few inches every time you do that.

The other thing about the compass is that if you get in a short tacking duel you have strongly in your mind what the proper course is on each tack. That way you can come through the tack and settle down on approximately the right compass course immediately and not have to grope around for it.

I think when you're tacking, especially in a fairly smooth sea, you want to come about quite slowly until you're head to wind. You sail it up into the wind and then bring her through fairly smartly but check your swing before you come down to the course or you'll be pulled on by. I don't think you should come through and then have to reverse the wheel. You want to come through stays and settle down pretty close to your proper course.

84

The Twelves are so heavy and so clean they carry an awful lot of way through. Most of the Twelves, Olin's especially, when they're being sailed properly, don't need to be rapped off before you start to come about. You can gain a few feet by holding her head to wind a little bit when you tack. That's if the fellows on the tacking line have your jib well forward so it's not aback on your shrouds like a brake. Snapping it around too fast or coming too slowly can lose too much way. It's the way that carries you through and if the boat slows down, that momentum has to be built up again.

Sailing in rough water is more complicated. In the confused sea you get from the spectator fleet, it's hard to tell what to do. You don't want to lift your bow over one sea and get her up too high and then get hit by three big seas because that will stop you dead. There are times when you might go off with a sea and then bring her up through smaller ones. If you can generally keep going in the direction you want and hit a reasonable number of seas the way you want to hit them, you're lucky. But you can't get them all.

I think the less you use the wheel the better off you are. Sailing any boat is a matter of anticipation. As you see the sea coming, you start to swing your boat before the sea gets there and you don't have to use much rudder. If you get thrown way off course and have to bring her back, then you have to use a lot more rudder. One thing that can help you minimize rudder use is to know your boat well: you may find that in a given sea she'll swing a little off course, but she'll come right back by herself without your sawing away at the rudder. I have always felt, and I was told by the little Scotsman who first taught me how to sail, that a good boat will go faster steering herself, or nearly so.

OLIN STEPHENS: The July trials were not too satisfactory from the Cup Committee's point of view, since six races were canceled because of fog or insufficient wind. But I was pleased with *Intrepid*. She won six races, and the important thing was she beat *Columbia* by more than three minutes in a good breeze and by over four minutes in light to moderate going. This was most encouraging because *Intrepid* is not at her best in the lower wind ranges. Bus got the start in both races and in the race where it was blowing about fifteen, the boat moved very nicely through the seas. *Columbia* carried quite a bend in her mast but I think our mainsail looked a bit better.

TOBY TOBIN: Our first race with *Columbia* in the July trials was in a

The 1967 defender was selected by the America's Cup Committee of the New York Yacht Club: (left to right) Julian K. Roosevelt, Henry Sears, Charles Francis Adams, Chairman Henry S. Morgan, Commodore Percy Chubb II, W. Mahlon Dickerson.

TOBY
TOBIN

twelve to sixteen knot southwester. We used our nine-ounce genoa and from the start had her under control. Briggs Cunningham let us get on his weather quarter on the wrong side of the line. Luffing nearly head to wind, Bus held his position beautifully for about three minutes. When Briggs broke his jib to jibe away, we broke ours, turned inside of him and forced him off down the wrong side of the buoy. We waited until we had a close reach to the mark before jibing and heading for it. *Columbia* ultimately started about forty seconds behind us. From then on we gained on every leg and won by three minutes and forty-five seconds.

86

A

The July Trials produced one of the most exciting starts of the summer (photographs a–f). In (a) the starting gun has gone, Intrepid and Columbia were well over the line, luffing almost head to wind.

Mosbacher holds Intrepid *on* Columbia's *weather quarter.*

C

Cunningham breaks out his jib and starts to swing back for the line. Intrepid swings inside . . .

D

... and carries Columbia *beyond the starting buoy.*

E

In complete control, Mosbacher jibes and heads back for the line with Columbia
directly astern. Intrepid *hardens up at the buoy . . .*

F

. . . and crosses the line with a sizeable lead.

Briggs did not attempt to engage us in a tacking duel, possibly because of winch trouble. They had two bad tacks, one a bad cast off and one a bad trim. Briggs seemed to be pinching more than we were and it hurt him. Bus did much better when giving the boat a good full rap, using the speed to take best advantage of our tab.

Seven Twelves participated in the New York Yacht Club Cruise, held between the Observation and Final Trials for the Cup boats. Jockeying at the start (left to right) Constellation, Nefertiti, Sceptre, *the British Challenger in 1958,* Weatherly, American Eagle, Intrepid. Columbia *cannot be seen here.*

95

The New York Yacht Club Cruise, which came shortly after the July trials, was not particularly eventful until the squadron run from Hadley's Harbor to Marion on August fourth. We later called this black Sunday—it was disastrous for the *Intrepid* Syndicate. Both *Constellation* and *Intrepid* lost their masts. *Connie's* broke halfway up because of upper spreader failure. Ours broke just above the lower spreaders at the joint, probably because of lower spreader failure. The wind was fresh but not enough to take the mast out, especially in the relatively quiet sea. This failure, our second, caused uncertainty, to say the least.

Bizzy, standing at the shrouds, lost his balance and fell overboard. He was quickly recovered by the tender. Bobby Connell lost his balance in the halyard hatch and fell on the shroud tie rod, injuring his back.

The fuss and furor you might expect in such a crisis just didn't happen. There wasn't a raised voice. Bus, remembering his loss of words on Long Island Sound, ordered "broken mast drill." The spar was taken on deck and stripped and we towed back to Padanarum.

BIZZY MONTE-SANO: I was coming aft and all of a sudden the boat straightened up and flipped me overboard. I was on the windward side and almost grabbed the shrouds. I was in the water maybe three to five minutes. They threw me a life ring from *Intrepid*. I swam over to it, but like most everything else on the boat the ring was quite small and light. It was quite a disappointment. While I was in the water *American Eagle* came by and asked if I needed help and I said no, I was fine. Then *Mary Poppins* picked me up.

PAT HAGGERTY: I was just a spectator on the boat the day it happened in Buzzard's Bay. I was in the corner of the cockpit trying to stay out of the way and I happened to be looking just below the spreaders. If I had been looking right at them, I might have known more. But the impression I had was clearly that the spreader let go first, and I told Olin this.

BUS MOSBACHER: After losing the masts we had *Intrepid* and *Constellation* back in commission in three days and we began our last scrimmage before the final trials. I was sure Olin had solved the problems, but in the back of my mind there was a trace of apprehension. I guess many of the crew had the same reaction, but we all more or less tried to ignore it.

We continued to work on our sails, the jibs and spinnakers. Teddy Hood spent a lot of time with us and with a little recutting he improved most of the genoas. He was still experimenting with our chutes and changing the shapes a bit so though they were flatter and had less draft they seemed to work better than some of the fuller sails.

I think the crew was in fine shape, but obviously anxious to get down to the short strokes and to accomplish what we set out to do.

TOBY TOBIN: After four days of the final trials, *Columbia* had the same record of three wins and no losses as we had, but that was because our race with her was canceled when the boats failed to finish within the time limit. *Intrepid* was ahead and that might have impressed the Committee, but it doesn't show in the record books. Then a scheduled layover day and two days of fog interrupted things for three days.

We finally got a shot at *Columbia,* and it was an interesting race. Bill Ficker was sailing her instead of Briggs and at the start he very neatly turned the tables on us after we nearly had him locked up. We forced through his lee and put him over the line about a minute and fifteen seconds before the gun. The idea was to carry him beyond the mark, jibe, come back, and recross ahead of him on port tack. But in bearing off, we got ahead of him, allowing him to turn and jibe inside us. So he controlled the start in a better position than ours. But after a series of tacks we worked into clear air and went rapidly into the lead. We beat him to the windward mark by about a minute. We gained slightly on each of the reaching legs but didn't do much on the next weather leg because we changed to a nine-ounce jib, expecting more wind, which didn't materialize. On the next run, *Columbia* cut our lead in half. It looked as if her spinnaker was a big one like ours but it stood much better and certainly helped her. I thought we should have tried another chute, since we lost very little on a change, but we stuck it out with the three-quarter-ounce runner.

On the final beat to the finish, we went back to a five-ounce jib and seemed to go twice as fast and regained a little more than our original lead, finishing a minute and thirty-nine seconds ahead.

BUS MOSBACHER: At the start we bore away to get back on the right side of the starting line and *Columbia* bore away behind us and trailing us. I think I could have safely jibed across her bow—and later Bill Ficker said he was sure we could have. I was ready to do it when suddenly I felt the wheels going around in my head, saying what the hell do you want to do that for? You have a good boat and a good breeze. Why take the chance? So we hung on and let Bill get the start. I think we could have

BUS
MOSBACHER
gotten away with it, but you must hold your ego in check. You hate like hell to get plastered at the start like that but, after the poor start, we went through eight or ten tacks and by that time we were in the lead and that's the name of the game.

Mosbacher was admittedly not aggressive on starts. Since he had a fast boat, his strategy was to stay out of trouble, keep his wind clear, and let Intrepid go. In this situation (a) he is astern, slightly to weather of Columbia; moments later (b) Intrepid is well to windward.

TOBY TOBIN: After our race with *Columbia,* the Cup Committee eliminated *American Eagle* and *Constellation.* I guess there was a certain amount of psychology involved. Since *Columbia* is a California boat the New York Yacht Club committee would make every effort to see that she got a fair shake. It didn't take long to prove this. The next day we took *Columbia* by seven minutes and forty-five seconds in a light northeaster that shifted into the east. The start was about even but we turned the weather mark with a lead of more than a minute and a half. We added about six minutes on the reaching leg and kept this margin upwind and down to the end of the race. Most of us thought this would settle it, but the Committee didn't see it that way.

We raced *Columbia* again the following day in a truer breeze, about a ten-knot easterly. *Intrepid* led by a over a minute and a half at the first mark. Bus built this up to almost four minutes at the finish.

As we came into our berth in the harbor, the little blue launch with Harry Morgan and the Cup Committee slid alongside *Intrepid* and Commodore Morgan solemnly informed Bus that *Intrepid* had been selected to defend the America's Cup. We'd been waiting for that all summer, and though we were pleased, most of us felt a sense of anticlimax.

The official launch bearing the America's Cup Committee comes alongside Columbia *to report their decision to terminate the Trials and select* Intrepid *as the defender.*

In a brief but always exciting ceremony, Cup Committee Chairman Morgan officially notifies Mosbacher that *Intrepid* has been selected to defend the America's Cup.

In *Intrepid's* cockpit, Strawbridge, Stephens, and Mosbacher celebrate the best news they have heard all summer with champagne in paper cups.

After *Intrepid's* selection, among the first visitors in her cockpit were Mosbacher's three sons (left to right) John, Bruce, and Trip.

With a 19–1 record in match racing (and the one loss due to a blunder) it was hard not to think that selection was merely a matter of time. Almost all of us had been involved before and this summer's campaign was very different from '58, '62 and '64. *Intrepid* was the only new boat this year and it was pretty clear early in the season that she was exceptional. The Syndicate was marvelously organized; the skipper, the acknowledged expert; the boat, the latest product of Olin's genius; and the crew, vastly more experienced than any of the others.

The mirth and hilarity of the evening's festivities were somewhat restrained. There were smiles and songs and champagne, but everyone felt a certain gravity. We had known long ago it would happen, and it finally did.

After our selection there was certainly no letdown. We practiced on a windward-leeward course between the torpedo buoys. In this short stretch we accomplished all the evolutions of the race course, only twice as fast and twice as often. The first time around was a bit slow, but as we warmed up we got better and better. The sense of being part of a well-drilled team had thoroughly penetrated each of us. Every maneuver, from raising the main in the morning to coming alongside the tender in the evening, was performed with a sharp efficiency that reflected our training. Each man had his position for each activity and each did his task with near-perfect timing and no waste motion.

VIC ROMAGNA: Here's the routine we developed for rounding the leeward mark. It was important to carry the spinnaker as long as possible but even more important to have it down as we started to windward. There was, therefore, great emphasis on speed in changing from chute to genoa.

In the preparatory stage Jory cleared the spinnaker foreguy from the genoa, while Bob changed the genoa sheets to the correct side of the spinnaker pole (both necessary if we'd had an odd number of jibes since setting the chute). Toby eased the mainsail leech line and took the main outhaul out to the mark. Meanwhile, Bizzy, the tailers, and grinders were trimming the spinnaker. George and I trimmed the main. Bus quietly steered for the mark.

Then Jory released the genoa halyard tie-down and the two stops holding the sail on deck. Simultaneously, George in the cockpit was setting up the weather-running backstay, I prepared to release the boom vang, and Toby passed the genoa halyard tail to Bob. As Bizzy yelled, "Let's go on the jib," Ned Hall tailing and Sam Wakeman grinding took the spinnaker pole far enough off the headstay to allow the genoa hanks to clear, and Bob, Jory, and Toby hand-over-handed the jib. At this point everything happened at once. Billy Kelly tailing and Dave Elwell grinding trimmed the genoa, and Toby went below to winch the genoa halyard, which Bob tailed with one hand. Jory went forward on deck to disconnect the guy from the spinnaker, which was lowered to him by Bob's other hand. I dove forward and below to ease the spinnaker halyard and George was there, too, to pull it down as soon as Jory disconnected. Meanwhile Bizzy was lowering the pole and Ned was taking the mainsheet onto his winch drum for the rounding. George, Bob, and Toby horsed the spinnaker down and Jory jumped below to help Sam crank in the mainsheet. When the pole was down, Bizzy helped overhaul the mainsheet on deck. When the spinnaker was down, Toby helped David trim the jib and I went aft to take the main back to its own small winch. The coffee grinders were then linked together for windward work and we were ready to tack within a couple of lengths of the mark. George set up the permanent backstay and Toby set the odometer.

Trimming the main and jib during the rounding was critical. Too fast or too slow—either would kill boat speed. As we rounded up the sails had to come in, trimmed to the point of sailing the boat was on. We did this hundreds of times and it always worked, and our total time was less than a minute.

In those final days before we met *Dame Pattie* we perfected every maneuver until it was executed with robot-like precision. Physically and psychologically we were ready for the Aussies.

Early in the season on the Sound Constellation sharpened her skills against her 1964 rival, American Eagle. In a moderate breeze, the Bird leads as McCullough tries to work out to windward.

The Trial Horse　　　　　5

BUS MOSBACHER: *Constellation* was supposed to be a trial horse for us, a sort of second string to the bow in case *Intrepid* wasn't as good as the tank led Olin to believe. Also, having *Constellation* in the Syndicate allowed Olin to try this departure in design, which I don't think he was sure about. If we had not had *Constellation, Intrepid* might have been just a refined copy of *Constellation*.

BOB MC CULLOUGH: I first thought of doing something about a 12-Meter —not necessarily participating in it personally—when I read of the sale of *Constellation* to the French. I thought that was a shame because it might well be the best boat that could be designed, or at least as good as any new boat and perhaps better. I was on the Board of the New York Yacht Club at the time and I figured we should put up the best possible defense of the Cup. Even if a new boat was coming along, *Connie* could help you find out whether she was as good or better.

So through Sparkman & Stephens's yacht brokerage office, Bob Garland and I made arrangements to contact Baron Bich in France. Bich came over here and we discussed the possibility of chartering *Constellation*. He indicated they would be interested. Then I had lunch with Rod and Olin and Rod told me of their commitments to the new Syndicate, which was to be known as the *Intrepid* Syndicate. He also

McCullough, a highly successful cruising-boat skipper, quickly adapted to sailing a Twelve.

BOB
MC CULLOUGH

spoke of their commitments to a West Coast group. I guess Olin had suggested some design modifications for *Columbia* before he became wholly involved with *Intrepid*. Anyway, Rod made it clear they couldn't do any design work for me if I brought *Constellation* back.

It seemed to me that it was absolutely ludicrous to think of going into the serious business of defending the Cup without having the designer in your corner. It didn't make any sense at all, and it would have made less sense to get a new designer to compete with all the tank-testing Olin had done. To me, it pretty much ruled out bringing *Constellation* back. I had just about reached that decision when Bus, not knowing of my attempt to bring *Constellation* back, asked me to join him in the *Intrepid* endeavor. At that point I had a brainstorm—why not put the two boats together so that the Syndicate would have two strings to its bow. If disaster should overtake *Intrepid, Constellation* might still be good enough to defend the Cup and, if *Intrepid* didn't prove as good as *Constellation, Connie* might be the ideal boat to defend.

Olin was first to agree that because a boat looks better in the tank doesn't mean she's going to look better when she gets into the water. At that time there was a real chance *Constellation* might be better than anything else, because we hadn't made a breakthrough with the new *Intrepid* design. So we decided to put the boats together.

Originally I had planned to start a syndicate to bring the boat back but I didn't have any syndicate members lined up because I didn't want anyone to get involved until I made sure, number one, that I could get the boat and, number two, that I could get the designer. When I couldn't get the designer, I never went any further as far as a syndicate was concerned.

Very early in the game I had taken an option to charter *Constellation* and went from there to a discussion of whether they would be reasonable in price—and they were reasonable, I guess, though in the end, they should have paid us for taking over the boat and putting it back in shape the way we did.

Before *Intrepid* was completed and in the water I thought *Constellation* was a definite defense candidate. Particularly so until we ran into the new breakthrough on the underbody of *Intrepid*. Once I saw what her underbody was like in the tank I was most enthusiastic about her and realized we had a real new boat. I think we still don't know everything there is to know about *Intrepid* by a long shot. I think she's going to be even faster next time.

After sailing against *Intrepid* day after day on the Sound, I knew in the bottom of my heart that only if disaster should befall *Intrepid* could *Constellation* defend the Cup.

When we found out in June that *Constellation* wasn't as fast as *Intrepid,* we had to decide whether to just go along with a skeleton crew and use her as a trial horse to tune *Intrepid* or to consider her as a potential defender. There were a couple of things about that. The Cup Committee really wanted all four boats out and they would have been very unhappy about putting her to bed—and we didn't know what a kicker would do for *Connie. Columbia* had a kicker put on and *Dame Pattie* had one so we thought we'd better find out if *Intrepid* would still be better than *Constellation* if *Connie* had a kicker; maybe the kicker was the answer to the whole thing. On the other hand, the Syndicate had already spent more money than they had planned to, so we made a deal that if I paid to put on the kicker, which I thought the boat should have, they'd keep her going.

Connie *had no trouble with* **Weatherly,** *who began to show her age despite Cunningham's expertise.*

BILL STRAWBRIDGE: Originally Harry Morgan wanted to have some trials in the Sound in June. Bus was not in favor of that. He felt he could do more tuning up the boat without actually racing. But when they got *Eagle* out and the *Columbia* boys chartered *Weatherly,* we couldn't do much but go with it. Actually, Olin and I felt the tuning up of the new boat had progressed far enough so that a little formal racing would be good for the crews. After that, *Constellation* was so valuable to us that we decided to take her to Newport for the trials there. Again the Cup Committee put the heat on us because they wanted four boats there so they could pair off for the trials.

Intrepid felt the pressure from her stable-mate all summer long. Both boats were fairly evenly matched off the wind, and as McCullough begins to overtake him Mosbacher prepares to jibe.

BOB MC CULLOUGH: After we put the kicker on *Connie* and found in the July trials that *Intrepid* was still faster, I realized more than ever that we were certainly a trial horse and not a candidate, but I was determined to get *Constellation* going her absolute best in case something happened to *Intrepid*. We had spent all this dough and it would have been a shame to have it go down the drain; just as important, it made sense to keep *Intrepid* on her toes all the way. Consequently, we didn't give up for a minute. We really went after them, and the crew's morale and spirit were terrific. They believed they could give *Intrepid* a good run for her money and if she stubbed her toe at all, they would be in.

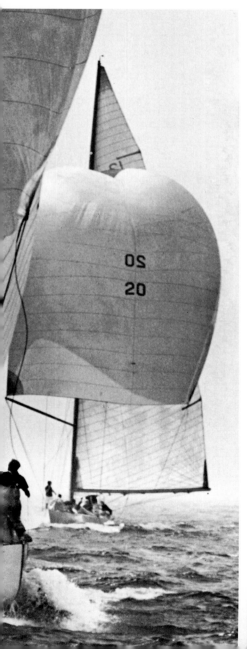

I was a little worried about morale in the beginning. I felt that maybe the crew would begin to figure they were on the second team, that they'd be disappointed and their disappointment would be reflected in their performance. I guess I worried a little more than I had to. One of the big things was the business of the crews being together at Eastbourne Lodge. The fellows on *Intrepid* never made the guys on *Connie* feel that they were their juniors. It was all one big party and that helped a lot.

We set up a friendly rivalry between *Intrepid* and *Constellation.* And we had a few gimmicks like taking off the Syndicate jerseys and putting on our own every time we raced the *Intrepid* gang. We let them know early in the game we weren't going to be their batboys.

TOBY TOBIN: Bob McCullough got his crew well wound up. They became real competitors but they were in a tough position. If they had something we needed and there was only one of them, we got it. Most of the time they performed for our benefit. Occasionally, we performed for theirs, but more often than not they did what we requested for the benefit of *Intrepid's* training.

They were certainly invaluable to us. I don't think any other candidate has had the benefit of having the previous defender as a trial horse. We made few crew changes on *Intrepid,* but there was always some kind of nervous joking about *Connie's* crew being ready to step in if we looked tired. I don't think any of us thought about that seriously, but it was lurking in the backs of our minds.

Both crews lived in the same house and though each person clearly thought of himself as a crew member on *Intrepid* or *Constellation,* he also thought of himself as a team player and some deep personal relationships developed over the summer.

BUS MOSBACHER: *Constellation's* crew had a great sense of loyalty. There was one occasion when a crew change was being made on *Intrepid* and I offered the job to David Rockefeller. He said he thought there were other people who could take the job I had in mind, but he didn't know who could step in and do his job on *Constellation.* He wasn't being boastful, just honest and realistic. I think it's quite a thing when a guy out of loyalty to the trial horse would give up a job on *Intrepid.*

BOB MCCULLOUGH: Any time we could do something better than *Intrepid* the fellows took great pride in it. We did come up with some

Constellation's *crew*: (*standing*) *John Browning, Norris Strawbridge, Richard duMoulin, Thomas R. Young, Skipper Robert W. McCullough, Richard Strawbridge, G. West Saltonstall;* (*kneeling*) *George O'Day, David Rockefeller, Jr., Gerald Y. Silverman, Daniel P. Brown.*

inventions or devices that were used on *Intrepid,* and that gave the fellows a kick too. One of them, for example, was a little thing, a device, for putting rubber bands we used for stops on the jibs. The bands were slipped onto a small section of hollow aluminum mast and as the furled jib was pulled through the hollow section, the elastic stops were flipped off onto and around the sail. It's a little difficult to explain, but it worked, especially with hankless sails. Most of the time on our sails with hanks the bands would stick on the hanks if they were put on in the usual way. But using *Connie's* mast device, the bands broke off and made a cleaner job of breaking out the jib.

We also had a hand in developing a spinnaker that was later used more than any other spinnaker by *Intrepid.* This was a big reaching chute that was developed first by cutting down one of *Constellation's* old running spinnakers and reshaping it. But Teddy Hood got his signals crossed and also made a new spinnaker to the dimensions of the cut-down one. This sail arrived with *Constellation's* numbers on it. We gave it to *Intrepid* to try and they liked it so much it became her main chute when reaching or running in a heavy breeze. This was the so-called "mystery chute" and it was typical of some of the things that gravitated from *Connie* to *Intrepid* as the result of our constant effort to improve the trial horse.

BILL STRAWBRIDGE: They stripped a lot of stuff off *Connie* up in Newport. Bob had contacted Baron Bich, who was there at the time, and he said, "Sure, go ahead." So Bob and the crew went to work and chopped out excess woodwork and everything else Bob Blumenstock, the measurer, would allow. That enabled them to add ballast. That and the kicker and new sails greatly improved the boat. We got her a new mainsail, a nine-ounce one, and it was far better than the twelve-ounce mainsail.

BOB MC CULLOUGH: We took off some four hundred pounds of weight at one crack. Eventually, we removed enough to be allowed to put back a thousand pounds of ballast, which definitely helped *Connie's* performance and made her stiffer. We also got some of the gear to work better, and all these things gave the crew incentive to keep improving her.

Our boys got a great kick out of racing *Intrepid*. In smooth water there was not much difference between the two boats. Going downwind, they were just about even and in broad reaching again it was a toss-up. Going to windward, even in a swell, *Intrepid* was better, but not too much better. But going to windward in a breeze and a chop, she was substantially better, better than any of the other Twelves, too. That's where she was a real breakthrough.

On the starts I had to be aggressive. Bus had a winner and his business was not to get in trouble. If I had been in his spot, I probably would have done the same thing. If you've got the fastest boat you want to keep your skirts clean. On the other hand, we spent hours and hours of practice on starts. In the actual races *Intrepid* never had to show what she could really do in maneuvers before a start. She was absolutely fantastic. It is just too bad people couldn't have seen what happened when we got into those roundy-go-rounds and how fast that boat could turn and what potential she had.

Bus never had to use that and really just tried to stay clear of his opponents. As a result of all the practice I got fighting for my life, which is just what I was doing most of the time with *Constellation,* we became pretty adept at staying out of trouble and keeping on our feet and ready to go at the right time. I think the practice may have helped us more than it did Bus.

GEORGE O'DAY: Throughout the spring, I was on *Intrepid* and all of a sudden, as he often does, Bus made a major decision. He said, "George, if *Connie* is going to be any good to us at all, I'll have to put you over there, because you are the only one with 12-Meter experience. You can help train the crew or we'll never know if our boat is going well or not." Bus also indicated that I was to have considerable time on the wheel, but Bob McCullough never let go of it.

BOB MC CULLOUGH: I suppose one of the things Bus and the Syndicate wanted in the worst way was a back-up skipper, and that is one reason why he got me and George O'Day. We all agreed that when the Syndicate had spent this amount of money we'd have one, if not two, back-up skippers. That's one reason why I spent so much time, or practically all the time on *Constellation,* just keeping my hand in sailing the boat. Actually, we also had Teddy Hood. He agreed to sail if worse came to worst. As things turned out, we never needed a back-up man.

The Syndicate also faced a problem that had never come up before. In the past, most trial horses had been plugs which were not manned or maintained in peak condition. In '67 the Syndicate had what amounted to a reserve defender. But when they finally decided what *Constellation's* role was to be, it was a little late. They had backed into a bigger expense than they thought they were going to have. I think the Syndicate had two ideas. They said, "Well, we've got the best boat and even if we have a disaster, we can hop onto *Constellation* and work her up pretty quickly." Also, when they saw how much effort the boys were putting out and the spirit they had, they didn't quite have the heart to shut them off as quickly as they might have done earlier.

Obviously, they had thought of putting *Connie* away early in the game, and as a result there wasn't much money spent on us in the beginning. Because of crew changes, and because we didn't get all our sails until late in the season, *Constellation* didn't even come to her peak until the August trials. She was just starting to get there. We didn't even have our heavy-weather jib until the New York Yacht Club Cruise. By the time we got that cut down just right and everything else, we were well into the final trials. But the Syndicate really spent a lot of dough on us, and I don't have any complaints at all. Certainly, they did more than was bargained for, and I think maybe the timing was just a little off.

BILL STRAWBRIDGE: We gave *Constellation* what she needed, but she just didn't have a lot of back-up stuff. One thing that irked Bus, and I can't say I blame him, was that sometimes work had to be done on *Constellation* to get her out there and Bus wanted things done on *Intrepid* that didn't get done. But we couldn't just neglect *Constellation* and keep her going properly.

BOB MC CULLOUGH: Our equipment was good. *Intrepid's* winches were definitely better than ours. We had trouble with ours in the beginning. They were the first ones built that way and weren't kept up too well, but once we got the bugs out, they were perfectly satisfactory. They weren't quite as powerful as those on *Intrepid*, but, on the other hand, they had some features that were maybe better. We could back ours off. You don't have to do that very often, but if you ever get an override, it's awfully nice to be able to ease out. We could ease in or out with the fine trim vernier attachment on our winches and this never worked well on *Intrepid*.

The crews on the two boats had to be handled quite differently. Bus had a veteran crew. All but one had sailed on Twelves, they knew basically what had to be done. Their problem was a completely different layout—they had to work out methods of handling that. My problem was to train a crew that hadn't been on Twelves before and to get them ready so that they could sail *Constellation* the best way possible, and if and when they were needed on *Intrepid*, they'd be ready for that also. Bus had to handle his crew so they'd stay interested and not get cocky or complacent. He didn't have to expect mistakes, and I did. I had to put up with mistakes and coach the crew along so they gradually eliminated them.

We frequently had to supply *Intrepid* with crew members when their guys were sick or away. So I had one of my best men on the easiest job on *Constellation*. He was kind of my swing man, a jack of all trades, who could work amidships or navigate or whatever. When we had to put a man on *Intrepid*, my swing man would take his place and we'd bring in somebody from outside and put him in the easy job.

I had to learn myself as we went along. I had sailed on Twelves a little before the war but not since. It's quite different from handling a

114

Constellation and Columbia fought it out like this all during the trials. McCullough often led upwind only to lose his lead running. Although Constellation was eliminated before Columbia, she defeated Columbia in the Newport Cup Race.

cruising boat. The first thing I had to get used to was that it felt so good and so wonderful I couldn't believe anybody could beat us. When I found out that the other Twelves could go the same way, I had to concentrate on steering a very fine line. There's a knack to learning how far up to pinch her and still make her go. The boats go so darn fast you'd think you're doing just great and then you'd find out another fellow who wasn't pointing quite as high was actually making out better than you were. It's like getting the feel of a race horse and putting her through her paces—discovering how quickly she'd tack and how well she does when she's brought about. Twelves can be tacked too fast or too slowly—there's a fine knack to doing this and you have to get it down just right. Then too, I had to get used to having a crew that, once they learned the ropes, would come up with anything I asked of them. That is a kind of luxury I wasn't used to before.

Our boys were very unhappy when *Constellation* was eliminated before *Columbia*. In the first place, in not one race all summer did *Columbia* beat us to the windward mark the first time up. It was a light fluky summer and in a couple of races she caught us downwind when she came up with a fresh breeze. We felt that the Committee didn't take into consideration facts that were quite evident to other people. The crew thought we should have had at least one more crack at her and they were quite bitter when we didn't.

As the *Columbia* fellows told me later, there was no question about *Constellation* taking *Columbia* in a breeze. We did that on the New York Yacht Club Cruise, and any other time we got a breeze. On one run of the Cruise, we were ahead of *Columbia* when we had a jib sheet jam and had to cut it with wire cutters to clear it. Well, this got us behind her, but on one beat we not only caught up but gained over a minute and a half or two minutes on her in a breeze of about twelve to fifteen knots. The only way they could hold us was in light air, but then in the City of Newport race we beat her decisively in light air, so we felt we could beat her in any kind of going.

We had some exciting moments during the summer. I guess the one we remember most was when *Constellation* lost her mast on the Cruise, the same day *Intrepid* lost hers. Actually, we had been lucky. We had spreaders go five or six times and nothing happened to the mast. We originally thought the trouble was caused by poor welds and that perhaps the French hadn't treated the mast just right. One time we figured that one of our crew had pulled the backstay tight when it was caught around the spreader. Then they blamed the titanium and finally, of course, everyone realized it was spreader failure. This was not caused by stress but by a twisting force that developed from the way the spreaders were fastened on the mast. On *Constellation* we changed the ears that fastened the spreaders to the mast. To further eliminate any tendency to twist we beefed up that part right next to the mast with a wooden plug and there was no trouble after that.

Probably the high point of the summer for me was the day *Intrepid* was selected to defend the Cup. I guess my crew felt somewhat the same way, but I had been on the project almost from the beginning, and this was what Bus and Vic and I had been working for long before we ever got *Constellation* back and before it was even decided I was going to sail *Constellation*. So, having been part of the thing, I felt a great sense of achievement.

VIC ROMAGNA: *Connie's* crew had great *esprit de corps*. When they were eliminated and later when we were selected, there was no animosity or unhappiness. They had worked like beavers and loved doing it. We kept some of them on as alternates for the Cup Races. They were pretty sure they weren't going to get on *Intrepid,* but they were happy to stay around. In fact, most all of the crew stayed and watched the races and then helped us at night. I guess some of them did more work on *Intrepid* than we did. We were tired and more interested in resting. If it hadn't been blowing hard, we might have taken one aboard at a time. I wish to God we could have, but with the blow-type race we had, no one was going to move off *Intrepid,* you can be sure of that.

BOB MC CULLOUGH: You naturally like to be on the defender, but the way things worked out there is no question but that I had a great summer and learned an awful lot. I think the final arrangements to keep the crews intact and not shuffle them around was very wise. That was the only way to do it. Those who sailed on *Intrepid* all summer deserved to sail on her right down to the end.

I hope that in '70 I can do it again, if my business will let me get away.[1] It was a wonderful experience.

---

[1] McCullough heads a syndicate which is building a new 12-Meter as a candidate to defend the Cup in 1970.

The Cockpit Crew 6

VIC ROMAGNA: Bus sailed better with people he trusted. Teddy was one, I guess I was one, George was one. He liked to have them around because he could ask a question and know what kind of an answer he'd get. Even then he got snappish. I remember one race when everything was going delightfully and I said, "There doesn't seem to be any change in wind direction anywhere, we're still footing a little faster than the other boat and pointing a little higher and things look about the same." And Bus said, "Do you know what that is? That's a nothing report." This brought the house down because he said it in anger. He was saying I shouldn't have even opened my face, and to call it a nothing report made us laugh. From that point on, George and I would say to each other, "Okay, your turn to give a nothing report." This would break Mosbacher up, and all summer long it was "nothing" reports.

GEORGE O'DAY: My friendship with Bus goes back quite a ways, I guess to about 1939. When we were all in college we had some terrific competition in the intercollegiates and at race weeks on the Sound and at Marblehead. My brother was a classmate of Bus's at Dartmouth and we got to know each other through team racing. Then, Bus was an usher at my wedding, and he went to Bermuda when we went there on our honeymoon. In fact, Bus took my bride sailing when I went racing with Shorty Trimmingham in the International 14 dinghies. So, over the years, we've come to know each other pretty well.

BUS MOSBACHER: Victor and George were my cockpit crew. Toby, of course, as navigator, was part of the group, but he gave me a different kind of information. Vic and George functioned as a couple of pairs of other eyes. They were supposed to look through a three-sixty and watch for wind shifts or anything ahead or astern that might affect us. One or the other, and sometimes both of them would watch the other boat and tell me what they were doing and how we were going, in comparison with them. If the other guy tacked and there was any appreciable time before the word got to me, there was a loud and angry scream. And if I saw it first, they knew about it.

For his cockpit crew Mosbacher had two veteran sailors who were long-time friends—Viv Romagna (right) and George O'Day (left). With one facing forward watching the wind and wave conditions and the other facing aft where the competition generally was, they fed their skipper the kind of information he needed to make decisions.

VIC ROMAGNA: One of my jobs was to watch tactical maneuvers. I was responsible for keeping my eyes totally on our competitor. I would call a tack or jibe or whether he was going higher than we were or anything he was about to do. Other than that, I had to keep my eyes forward to see that nothing on deck was being fouled up, or if it was, to call out and try to cure it before it happened.

We always ran a very quiet ship. Sending orders forward—nobody shouted, nobody hollered. That wasn't wanted. Consequently, ideas or orders were passed forward or passed aft from forward very quietly, and I was the relay station for these.

Bus didn't like a lot of people to talk to. He tuned himself in to certain people. Anything else was terribly disturbing to him because he concentrated so hard, so it was either George or I who passed information to him.

Toby also supplied information. He had all the navigational courses in grease pencil on a plastic sheet. Bus would ask a question which Toby would answer: there was very little discussion. Bus would say, "When shall I tack?" and the answer would be "In four minutes," or "In three minutes if you want to be short," or "You have seven minutes to the layline."

GEORGE O'DAY: As we came close to the weather mark, providing we had to tack to round it, one of my jobs was calling the tacking angles to Bus. We had the angles painted right on the deck and I would call out when we had the mark at forty-five and fifty and sixty degrees. Toby would have told Bus what his tacking angle had been up the windward leg, usually about seventy-two degrees. I'd keep calling the numbers out to Bus and when he felt we were on the angle he wanted, he'd say "Ready about," and we'd go.

Before we got to the mark, of course, Vic and Bus and I would discuss what spinnaker we should use. Bizzy usually suggested one and then Bus would decide. From then on Bizzy and the foredeck boys handled things. The situation was a little touchy because of the close relationship between Bizzy and Bus. Bizzy would sort of bypass Victor and me in the chain of command and discuss things directly with Bus and if we thought there should be some change in the trim of the spinnaker, we'd suggest it to Bus and he'd pass it on to Bizzy. It was a strange bit of protocol we had to live with.

VIC ROMAGNA: There were times when the cockpit crew would discuss tactics: on turning a leeward mark three minutes ahead of the other boat, should we tack and hold it for a minute and a half and then tack again so that when he rounded the mark, we would be in a straight line between him and the next mark. Or should we continue on the same tack at the mark, or go out until the windward mark is on a relative bearing of forty-five degrees. This hopefully would have had us tacking fewer times than our opponent and it would enable us to cover him and slow down the tacking duel.

These weren't long discussions. They were ideas that Bus would either accept or reject, with a, "Well, I think I'll do this instead." We volunteered suggestions and he would analyze them quickly. There was a constant give and take of ideas. Our treatment of this guy was as a total master, and in concentrating on sailing the boat, he did not watch tactics. Because he was busy keeping the boat going, at certain times we had to feed him the potential value of a tack or a jibe. At that point he came alive to the need for a tactic, and he'd study it and then say "Yes" or "No" or "We'll wait till we get to this angle and then go."

Bus used us for ideas, but he made all the decisions. We worked as a total unit. That's what we were there for.

Intrepid was a fast boat, and our thinking about tactics was modified accordingly. If you cut down the tacking in a tacking duel you'd be much further ahead at the end of the windward leg, but if a guy could snow you into a quick-tacking duel all the way, you would probably stay even with him. There'd be no boat gain in that maneuver unless someone fouled up.

In one race with *Columbia,* we were ahead of her and wanted to see what *Intrepid* would do. We went into I don't know how many tacks. We just covered her tack for tack about every thirty seconds and we couldn't shake her—we didn't gain a darn thing.

In tacking, George or I would tell Ned Hall or Billy Kelly when to stop trimming the jib. We knew about where it should be in certain weights of wind, so we'd get the sail to what we considered almost the perfect point. Then Bus would finger it in or out with his hand signals. After that he took over on trim. If the boat felt good, he might trim the jib and main a little more and head a little higher. He'd watch his instruments, and if she began to slow down he cracked her off a bit.

The trim on the mainsail was handled the same way. We would get it in to what we thought was just about right and Bus would say, "Take another inch," or "Ease her an inch." When we got in a tacking duel, I'd ease it off six inches and then forget it. As soon as the tacking duel

Romagna and O'Day supervised the trim of sails up to a point. Mosbacher hand signaled final trim.

VIC
ROMAGNA   was broken off, we'd come in on the trim.

GEORGE O'DAY: Bus was like a computer we'd feed information to. He made his own decisions, which was the way it should be, but he wanted information, and only that which was pertinent to the situation. He wanted to know what was going on at all times. If we were changing something, that immediately took his mind off sailing and he wanted to know why we were doing it. Vic and I were called the Bobbsey Twins because we'd start to yack at each other and Bus couldn't hear us. Finally, when he couldn't stand it any longer, he'd say, "What are you two guys talking about, I want to be in on it." We usually told him to sail his boat and we'd let him know if we discussed anything important.

122

We developed a very close relationship with Bus in the cockpit—when he knew people as he did Vic and me, he knew he could trust them. We've sailed with him for years, and if we said *Dame Pattie* was going faster, he knew damn well she was going faster.

Before the start, it was pretty much Bus's ball game. In '62, it was quite a bit different. We discovered *Gretel* was a little faster than *Weatherly,* so the starts at first were the ring-around-the-rosy type—they are always dangerous, because you can get tagged out. You have to be careful because you're playing with the rules and you must have instant knowledge of exactly what is involved. But as the '62 series progressed, Bus was more inclined to give up the ring-around-the-rosy business and to plan and time his start so he'd be on the line at a predetermined spot. This is what he did in '67. Three or four hundred yards from the line he made up his mind just the position he wanted to start in.

Our two rudders were a great tactical weapon. Jock Sturrock found that out the first time we were in a ring-around-the-rosy maneuver on the starting line. He got on our stern and we came head to wind and tacked, and before he could come around and tack, we had jibed around and were coming back aboard him. Jock was still up in the wind and saw us coming and just pulled away in the nick of time. That was the last time for the ring-around-the-rosy.

Some people criticized us for our starts, but I believe we were right. Their misconception, as far as I'm concerned, was that they thought *Intrepid* could point unusually high. I don't think she could outpoint anybody, but she made less leeway, she didn't get pushed off. While another boat could be pointing higher, *Intrepid* could still work out to windward of her. So the idea was to keep her wind clear and let her go.

In his book *View from the Cockpit,* Bob Bavier says he tacked the 1964 defender in an arc of sixty-four degrees and sometimes got down to fifty-eight. Now, on *Intrepid* most of the time our tacking angle was seventy-two degrees. This varied with conditions, of course, and sometimes we got down to seventy, but we rarely tacked in sixty-eight degrees. It just looked as though *Intrepid* was pointing much higher. Matter of fact, I asked Jock Sturrock what he was tacking in and he said sixty-nine to seventy degrees. I told him he had us by two degrees, but we found tacking *Intrepid* in seventy-two degrees was where the boat was comfortable.

VIC ROMAGNA: *Dame Pattie* consistently pointed higher than we did, but it was silly. It was a mistake on Jock's part because the boat just didn't respond. She didn't go up, she slid. They never got her going fast enough. She heeled over a lot and while she pointed higher, she wouldn't end up any higher than we did.

TOBY TOBIN: George and Victor were primarily tactical assistants. I was charged with furnishing strategic information. Bus didn't ask them for advice—he normally expected information to come without a request. He didn't want opinions, just facts that would affect the decision-making process. But Bus would ask me specifics such as course or time to tack.

VIC ROMAGNA: George and I didn't just watch the boat race and talk with Bus. We handled all the lines controlled from the cockpit. I was mostly on the mainsheet, George was on the backstays and boom vang, and Toby helped on the mainsheet and boom vang. I was also the downstairs man on spinnaker take-downs. George went forward too and helped pull the chute in. At this point the under-deck winch grinders would be going full tilt and I had to slide on my belly under them and come up on the other side to reach the spinnaker. I literally had to dive under them and go through. Then, as soon as the spinnaker was gathered in, I had to rush back and work on the mainsheet.

Bus was just about as rough on us as he was on the crew. Quite frequently, to take me out of the cockpit, he would ask me to go look at the trim of the jib. I would go forward and stand by the mast as he came slowly up into the wind, watching to see if the sail was luffing all along the luff. I would check this for perfect trim and while I was forward, Bus would throw a tack. No excuses, I was supposed to be on the backstay. I might have been thirty feet away, but I had to get that backstay up. That was my job.

GEORGE O'DAY: We worked like a bunch of monkeys around that cockpit. But everything got to be automatic. Almost every motion on *Intrepid* was that way; it was part of Bus's training. You learned not to think— you did your jobs first and then thought about them, checked to see if they were done right.

One of my jobs was relieving Bus sailing *Intrepid* downwind, frequently when he wanted to rest after the first, hard, windward leg. I would sail her down near the leeward mark and Bus would take over for the jibe. It wasn't talked about much, but one of *Intrepid's* weak spots was running and reaching. She was not as fast as *Constellation*. When I was on *Connie* earlier in the season, I don't think there was a race that we didn't gain on *Intrepid* off the wind. Of course, that was probably because of *Intrepid's* high aspect ratio rig. In any case, it didn't make any difference. Today, the boats are sailing Olympic courses where there is more emphasis on windward work, and that's where *Intrepid* is great.

She was a cinch to steer and she was easy to surf. *Weatherly* was lousy in this area in '62, particularly in the second race, when *Gretel* surfed by her. I'm not sure whether this was a weakness of the boat or a weakness of Bus's. I don't know if Bus really is exhilarated by bringing a boat off a wave. Maybe it's not his cup of tea. For me, there's sheer ecstasy in getting a boat surfing, whether it's a 12-Meter or anything else. I love it, I light up when you lay the stern into the wave and get it to lift and then play the boat off the wave.

I think most big-boat skippers don't know how to surf because they haven't been involved in planing boats. But you take some of the Cal-40 skippers, they are in seventh heaven. As far as they are concerned their boats are just big dinghies and they have a whale of a time, while the conventional keel-boat skipper doesn't like it at all. You've got to love surfing and also know what to do with the wave.

BUS MOSBACHER: Victor and George had all kinds of shoreside responsibilities. Vic, of course, was my Executive Officer, as he had been on *Weatherly* in '62. He spent a tremendous amount of time recruiting and organizing the crew and then setting up time schedules for practice sailing. Handling the logistics of who was going to be there when on weekends during the spring of '67 was not easy. First, we had one boat and two crews, and then we had two boats and often less than two crews. It involved hundreds of phone calls and letters and the real prodding he had to do with some fellows to get their exam schedules or the number of weddings they had to be in or whatever it was that was interfering. But if I wanted to go sailing, I'd just tell Vic. I didn't have to call ten or fifteen people.

A little further along, as we began sailing *Intrepid,* Vic was charged with checking the mechanical needs and deficiencies which always show up in something new. When sails had to be moved Vic was the guy that told the crew to stop talking to the pretty girls on the dock and get off their duffs and lug the sails. Things like that aren't done unless somebody tells the crew to do it. He took a tremendous burden off my shoulders and gave me time to discuss weather or navigational problems with Toby or sails with Teddy Hood or something about the boat with Olin. Vic carried through continually. He was usually the first on board in the morning and the last off at night. He was never one to say, "We can do that tomorrow morning."

VIC ROMAGNA: I get a great kick out of organizing a boat for somebody—to see it come out as a near-perfect unit or a darn good unit or at least as a unit we could look back on with pride whether we won or not. I've sort of made a study of being a crew—I've skippered boats for any number of years, but I prefer organization. So, on *Intrepid,* after working on the crew set-up, I paid a lot of attention to the hull and rig. All summer long I spent endless hours going over the boat—the chainplates, the mast step, the rigging. Lots of little things. The chainplates went four different times. Once the port chainplate went and I was the only one who felt it go; I sensed a crack in the boat that hadn't been there before. That night I found the crack in the chainplate, and we welded it. After every hard race Chuck Saddler, *Intrepid's* marine construction technician, used to go over the chainplates with a purple die to pick up cracks. We even found one the night before the last race with *Dame Pattie.* It was my job to keep track of things like this when we were dockside.

GEORGE O'DAY: Bus gave me the responsibility for the sails—that was my duty, the whereabouts of the entire sail department. If they were being fixed, I made sure they were back, and if they weren't back, where they were. I got bypassed a couple of times and I spoke with Bus—after that, sails were never moved until I had physically checked them out. Every day before we got underway I ran down our sail checklist so I could be sure all the sails Bus wanted were on board."

Our close relationship with Bus inevitably created other responsibilities for Victor and me. These were personal, and emerged from the tremendous pressure this dedicated guy put on himself. A couple of times we got into difficult situations, like the night Bus heard that George Hinman had given one of *American Eagle's* light spinnakers to *Columbia.* Bus was incensed by this. *Intrepid* was admittedly a good boat, but we never stopped worrying about *Columbia.* She might have been a serious threat in light air and Bus couldn't figure out why *Eagle,* after she'd been eliminated, wanted to continue to battle *Intrepid.* So he was ready to sound off.

The cockpit crew did what they could to relieve Mosbacher of the pressure of the press, but some TV interviewers were lucky to catch the skipper.

It took three hours to save this situation—and I mean *three hours*. It started at ten o'clock at night at Eastbourne Lodge and was still going at one in the morning. It was just by the grace of God that Bus couldn't get anybody on the telephone. He tried, he dared us to try and we talked with him and he'd go back again to the phone. This went on and on, until finally he began to cool off and went to bed.

Even more critical was the measurement incident.[1] That was really tense, and I put my own friendship with Bus on the line. To this day, Vic says, "George, I don't know how you dared to do what you did." Actually, I was the one who got Jock and Bus to meet in a Newport drug store and settle their differences.

[1] See page 147 for details of "the measurement incident."

In addition to all the other pressures Bus had to endure, there was the press. This built up from a ripple in June '67 to a tidal wave in September when the wire services and television crews piled into Newport on top of the throng of newspaper and magazine people already on the scene.

During the early trials, life was quite bearable. After we got in from a race, three or four yachting writers whom Bus had known for years would come down on the dock, chat briefly with him, and ask a few questions. That was that. They were knowledgeable guys, most of whom had watched the afternoon's proceedings, and they only needed a quote or two from the skipper around which to build their story.

The final trials, which started August 15, brought in a whole new batch of reporters. Naturally, every one of them wanted a personal interview with Bus, and he said, "Oh, gee, do I have to? Why don't you talk with them, George?" So from time to time, I tried to cope with the press so Bus could get off the dock without being hounded all the way to Thames Street. The Syndicate had the services of a public relations company and they acted as far possible as a liaison with the press. They prepared fact sheets, scheduled interviews, and tried to help the newsmen and protect Bus at the same time. It wasn't easy.

Once *Intrepid* was selected, we were blitzed by hard-nosed crews of camera and sound men. Finally, when it became difficult to get up and down our own dock, the gate to the pier was locked and the press was admitted by appointment only. We tried to be as understanding as possible. Olin Stephens submitted to questioning by a young lady from *Women's Wear Daily*. I never did read what she told her readers about the America's Cup Races.

As we approached the start of the Cup Races, the pressure from news media continued to mount. The phone at Eastbourne Lodge started ringing around seven in the morning and frequently people tried to reach Bus as late as twelve o'clock at night. Calls came in from London, Australia, California, and a dozen places across the country. They all, of course, wanted to speak with Bus. In most cases, the Syndicate's press relations people took the calls so Bus could finish his breakfast or dinner. The world-wide interest was astounding. There were correspondents not only from Australia but from France, England, and Canada. In addition to the Associated Press and United Press International, there must have been representatives from over a hundred American papers.

In spite of the added distraction and tension they caused, Bus did a number of television interviews. Usually they were shot from the dock with Bus in *Intrepid's* cockpit. Bus would stand patiently while the sound man got the level right, then the commentator asked him some questions, such as whether he thought *Intrepid* was the fastest Twelve ever built and then the director would say, "Please, Mr. Mosbacher, put your hand on the steering wheel." Throughout all this, there wasn't a flicker in Bus's famous smile, but I knew he was fuming inside and had to use the utmost control to put up with these shenanigans. That's one of the crosses a Cup Defender skipper has to bear.

It was a rare privilege to work closely with Olin and it was rewarding to see the dedication of the boys who worked on *Intrepid* and *Constellation*. They were never satisfied until things were just right. I enjoyed just being with a group of guys who were so uniquely motivated by the love of sailing. They all put out to the *n*th degree and that developed a sense of great cohesiveness among us. We achieved a degree of closeness and mutual respect that was intensely stimulating.

Even when *Vim* failed to be selected in '58, I looked back on that happily. Everyone on board had a feeling of satisfaction because they had given everything they had to give, and that was just as important to us as winning. The fact that *Intrepid* won put the icing on the cake, but the real reward was in the effort itself and in the sharing of the wonderfully close association with the superb *Intrepid* men and their ladies.

Following each Cup Race with *Dame Pattie,* press briefings were held in the Newport Armory. Newsmen submitted written questions to a moderator who screened them to eliminate duplication and inappropriate subjects. In '67 Bob Bavier, the skipper of the previous Defender, was the middleman, just as Bus had been when Bob won the Cup in 1964. At past briefings the skippers had answered the questions, but in '67 Bus balked at the idea. I didn't blame him and neither did Strawbridge. After hours of strenuous concentration, it was hardly reasonable to ask a skipper to face the TV lights and grinding cameras.

The New York Yacht Club Committee tried to get Bus to appear at the briefings, and he finally agreed on the condition that Jock would also be on hand. Then, apparently, Jock demurred and it was finally decided to have a member of the afterguard act as spokesman for each boat. I was tagged to field the questions for *Intrepid* and Norm Wright was there for *Dame Pattie*. Norm was a good choice because he had sense of humor. He sure needed it after we beat him by almost six minutes in the first race. He had to face some brutal questions and about all he could say was that they were looking for lighter weather. According to reports, *Dame Pattie* had been designed for an average breeze of about eleven knots and that first day it blew fifteen to eighteen knots.

For the second race the wind ranged from about seven knots at the start to fourteen knots at the finish. At the briefing, he was asked if that was *Dame Pattie's* weather and Norm could only say they wanted it lighter still.

The briefings were pretty routine and were supposed to be limited to one hour, but they always dragged on, with lots of supplementary questions from the floor. I was glad to save Bus from this ordeal. Even then he had to run the gauntlet of reporters who followed him from the pierhead gate to where his car was parked.

After we won the fourth race and the series, the skippers appeared at the briefing by prearranged agreement. Jock looked pretty somber and Bus, somewhat relaxed at last, appeared to be none the worse for being the first man thrown overboard at the dockside victory celebration. Questions from the newsmen were academic by then. The only one with prophetic import was addressed to Bill Strawbridge, who sat with Bus in front of the microphones. There had been rumors that the French wanted to buy *Intrepid,* and Bill was asked if she would be for sale. He replied with an emphatic "No." The *Intrepid* crew, bubbling with champagne supplied by Burr Bartram and the Newport Shipyard, provided appropriate background noise.

The Skipper 7

BUS MOSBACHER: Dad put me in a sailboat when I was four or five years old. I started in a small catboat and sailed many hours each day all summer long for several years. I didn't do much competitive sailing until I was ten or eleven years old. In those days the junior programs were few and far between and there weren't many youngsters in them. So I spent a lot of time just being in a boat. My brother Bob, who was five years younger than I, ultimately started the same way.

When I was ten or maybe just eleven, Dad bought Howie McMichael's Star boat for me and I went out to race in September just before going away to school. There was only one other Star out that day. It was *Old Sol,* sailed by Howie Walden, who, incidentally, is still sailing Stars. We started the race and Howie got well ahead of me. Then a tugboat and barge came across the course. The young fellow with me knew quite a bit about sailing. He told me to hold my course and head straight for the turning mark. I thought for sure we were going to hit the barge but it was out of our way by the time we reached it. Meanwhile, Howie had had to luff up to get around the barge and that put him behind us. So, with luck, I won my first race.

Subsequently, I did reasonably well in the Star Class, but we certainly didn't beat Adrian Iselin, the Atkin brothers, and people like that in the beginning. I remember I got the world's worst starts. They were so bad that even when we finished well, the newspaper report said we did well "in spite of a late start." Dad sailed with me occasionally, and he had no patience with this at all.

I raced in the Midget Championships in 1935 and 1936 and at the end of '36 or early '37 I got an Atlantic and sailed that for three years. My brother Bob inherited my Star. I also spent some time crewing for my dad on the Sound Interclub he bought when I was six years old. While I was still sailing my Atlantic, Dad bought an International One–Design and ultimately I graduated to that.

As I grew up on the water, two men had a tremendous influence on me. My dad, of course, was one, and the other was Peter Hansen, a middle-aged Scotsman who worked as a professional on our Interclub.

Dad was a martinet, if that's the word for a man with strong convictions, inflexible determination, and a Prussian sense of discipline. He had always been a pretty intense competitor, a good athlete and a fine golfer. He sailed the Interclub during the 1930's and did moderately well for someone relatively new to the sport. It used to bug him because he thought he didn't sail to windward as well as he should, but he always loved to handle a boat downwind. In recent years, we have kidded Dad by calling him the "George O'Day of the '30's," because

Mosbacher has been winning boat races with remarkable regularity ever since he started sailing in the Midgets. His most impressive performance was in the International One–Design class. He sailed Susan to eight season championships against some of the best skippers in the East.

George is known for his downwind helmsmanship.

As Bob and I did more sailing, Dad did less. He finally bought a 38-foot Matthews cruiser from Rudie Schaefer, who had used it to commute to the World's Fair in 1939. After that he hardly sailed at all. He just went out and watched us. He would watch me start in the Atlantics and follow along until I did something that annoyed the hell out of him. Then he'd take off and go back and watch how Bob was doing. A little while later, I'd see that bow wave and I'd know Bob had blown something and Dad was coming back to scout me.

Dad's race-course observations were aired at the dinner table in some pungent question-and-answer periods. There was hardly a race when we didn't have to explain why we did what we did—and not just if one of us had made a mistake. If you won a race by two miles by going off somewhere, he wanted to know why. Even if it was right, there had to be a good reason for it. It wasn't good enough to say "Because Mr. Shields or Mr. Knapp did," that wasn't an adequate answer because then he'd have to know why *they* did it, and Dad would say "You're not going to get anywhere by following other people all the time."

There were some times when I made inexcusable mistakes and I just didn't come home to dinner. I'd bunk with some sailing friends for the weekend. But even if I didn't get home until Tuesday night, I would still have to face the inevitable questions.

Dad was not as expert in some areas as Peter Hansen and other more technically oriented sailors, but he was a highly intelligent person and a very careful observer. In eight or ten years of tireless watching, he had learned a great deal about boat racing. If a boat went faster than mine, he would not attribute it to a lucky puff. That was a possibility, but if someone was consistently beating me, there had to be a reason. He didn't always have it, but if Bob or I were to continue to race, he expected us to address our attention to the problem and try to figure it out. Was it better sails, was our opponent steering better, was he trimming differently, was his bottom cleaner?

In Dad's book, we were expected to have a working knowledge of what the current was doing, what the wind conditions were, and what the weather reports projected. We didn't just run down and jump on our boats. Dad felt that the opportunities for sailing should be treated with respect and intelligence. He always had the feeling that if you're going to race, race. If not, then try something else. He always enjoyed doing something well and he said you can't do that unless you work at it.

He was a stickler for doing things the right way. One day he raced with me in the Star on the last day of Manhasset Bay Race Week, and we were ahead in a race we needed to win the series. Dad said, "I see you haven't replaced the jib sheets as I told you to." I replied that I had thought they were good enough. He said, "No, they're not," and he pulled out his knife, leaned forward, and cut the sheets. We lost the race. He made his point. Later he said, "Maybe you thought that was a stupid thing to do, but I wanted to teach you a lesson. I think you've learned it." Neither of us has ever forgotten that.

EMIL MOSBACHER, SENIOR: As a kid, Bus was always serious. He had a fine brain and was a *cum laude* student, but I wanted him to have other interests besides books. That's why I encouraged him to sail.

As he grew up, there were two ideas that conditioned my attitude towards him. Although I was only twenty-five years old when Bus was born in 1922, I had been very successful in business and I was determined not to have him spoiled by good fortune. Also, as my eldest son, I saw him as the one who would follow in my footsteps, the one whom I would depend on in future years. So I treated him accordingly. I was always rough on him. I always put things on the line with him.

When Bus was ten years old, I sent him to prep school. His mother didn't like the idea, but I felt I had done the right thing. I was sure he wouldn't get spoiled in a crowd of five hundred boys. Even as a youngster, Bus was very mature. In spite of stern discipline he never rebelled. I didn't dominate him and he always maintained his own strong individuality.

I got Bus the Star because the competition was tough in that class. He'd come up so fast in sailing I wanted him to go out and get his brains beaten out. I don't know whether that was right or wrong, but it was the way I looked at life.

Maybe I was an unusual father, but I guess other people have been the same way. While Bus was growing up, I read a book about the father of Suzanne Lenglen, one of the great tennis players of all times. He was very severe and strict with his daughter and I admired that. I admired the girl too. She conducted herself well and was quite a great person.

In World War II, Bus volunteered for the Navy and ended up on a minesweeper and that annoyed me no end. I had thought it would have been much better if he had gone in later when he was older and had had more training. Anyway, Bus was there in the thick of some of the nasty Pacific action, but he came out of it all right. When he got home, he didn't want to race any more. I don't know why, unless he'd had enough responsibility in the service to last a kid of twenty-one for a while.

Then Corny Shields telephoned me and said he wanted Bus to skipper one of the Internationals in a team race against Bermuda. I talked with Bus. It was one of our typical one-sided conferences. Bus was always a respectful listener, and finally he agreed to go, and the United States team won. A similar thing happened when he was asked to represent the Seawanhaka Yacht Club in the International 6-Meter races at Cowes, England. We had another conference and again I persuaded him to go and again he won. After that he campaigned *Susan* regularly and won eight International Class Championships against such fine skippers as Shields, Arthur Knapp, and Bill Luders.

Some people have given me credit for the qualities Bus and his brother Bob possess, but I've always said they came from the prep school masters who had a lot to do with bringing them up.

Bus's tastes have always been simple. He was brought up in the country and he preferred Dartmouth to other Ivy League colleges. He has always been frugal, even to the point of not buying new jib sheets. And above all, he has been a perfectionist. That's why he has always had such relentless drive.

BUS MOSBACHER: I was about ten years old when Peter Hansen came to work for Dad. In those days most of the Sound Interclubs had a professional hand, something quite different from today. All through the week I spent endless time sailing with him and talking with him. He was a fascinating fellow with a thick Scots brogue. If I hadn't spent days and weeks with him I would never have been able to understand him. I don't think Mother and Dad ever did get to understand him very well. But he was a man, then in his 50's or 60's, who had spent his entire career on sailing vessels. He'd gone to sea in his early teens on a square-rig ship and had had a full, deep sea experience. He knew just about everything there was to know about sailboats. I've worked with some great yachting technicians in recent years, and I have realized now how many things he knew just by the seat of his pants, from long experience. He couldn't explain the aerodynamics of sailing, but he knew what was right and worked terribly hard at teaching us these things. He had tremendous patience in answering questions.

Like so many old sailors, he was a great storyteller. He would ramble on about how he sailed on King George V's *Britannia* and about British-American team races on the Clyde. He also captained square-riggers and commercial vessels and he told one unforgettable story about a

135

merchant voyage. On passage from Australia to China, some of his crew got drunk, although he was certain there was no liquor on board. Finally, he found the men were tapping an oblong barrel that contained alcohol. Peter explained that the barrel not only contained alcohol but the body of a Chinese being returned to his homeland. That put an end to drunkenness in the crew.

Peter was eager to experiment and had a great feel for what made a boat go through the water. He had understood such things as light sail cloth, light sheets on your jib, proper vanging, clean bottom, and the balance of a boat. He never explained that the balance theory of a boat was a matter of center of efforts or anything like that, but he knew that if a boat was not tuned so that it virtually sailed itself, it wasn't going right. He acquired this through trial and error and he worked with me on sail trim and balance. He pointed out one very well known sailor on the Sound and said in his opinion he really wasn't very good because he had a heavy hand on the tiller. Someone who used a heavy hand on the tiller was really not part of his boat: he wasn't getting the most out of it.

Peter was absolutely tremendous in any kind of weather, but especially in light fluky weather. He had the patience of Job, except that he had absolutely no patience if I lost patience. He never put it into so many words or said you had to concentrate, but he often made it quite plain that he thought you were doping off: "What's the matter with you, don't you see that southerly coming in now?" or "There's a puff up there, what have you been thinking about?" or "Why aren't you looking for it?" or "Your jib's luffing, don't you know what's going on around you?"

Peter was a dedicated man, and we used to kid him about it. When we sailed on the Interclub and something had to be done, he'd step on anybody's feet. My father was his boss, but that didn't make a darn bit of difference. If Dad was in the way, he'd get an elbow in the ribs or his foot stepped on just as quick as anyone else—Peter would get to the sheet or whatever needed attention. He didn't go around people, he went right over them. He had the idea that if you're racing, you're racing. If you didn't want to race, then go cruise somewhere but don't mix the two.

I sailed with him about four years, from ten to fourteen. He was a great character and when I had boys of my own, I was sorry I didn't know someone quite like him when he was younger. When Peter came to us, he was an older man, which may have had something to do with it. He was a complete gentleman in every way. I never remember him using foul language or even doing or thinking anything improper. I'm afraid in this day and age he would be referred to as a straight arrow or a square. His dedication was to sailing and to boats and to maintaining them properly. He had no more patience with a sloppily kept boat than he did with a sloppily sailed race. If you got a good bottom on a boat, you kept it, and if you had a good sail, you treasured it. Of course, those were the old cotton sails, which were much more destructible than Dacron. My heavens, years before anyone thought about folding or caring for sails Peter was giving ours great attention, especially if they were new sails and good ones. In those days you spent twenty to twenty-five hours reaching gently across the breeze to break in a cotton sail.

Unless there was a lot of salt in it, it was absolutely forbidden to wash a new sail. Cotton sails had some kind of finish or dope on them and once you washed them you took some of the finish off the cloth and weakened it a bit. To Peter, this was maltreating a prized possession. And, of course, you never took your good racing sail just to go out sailing.

There was nothing slapdash or lazy about Peter. We sailed out of Mamaroneck and he came to work from Brooklyn every morning and went home every night, but he was never in any rush to leave. He was dedicated to his work. If the bottom needed sanding and painting, he did it, even if it took several extra hours. He was always in fine physical condition and at fifty-five or so he went hand-over-hand up the mast of an International without puffing. Peter came to my office late in 1967 when he was over eighty-six years old and his eyes were quite poor and his hearing nearly gone. He came over to me and said, "Emil,"—as he always called me—"you feel if I'm still in good shape." I felt his biceps and it was still hard as a rock. Peter died about a year later. He was a great character, a fine person and I hope some of his qualities have rubbed off on me.

I am convinced that my small-boat sailing experience was wonderful training for sailing a Twelve. A man who can sail a frostbite dinghy well can sail anything well. I don't think the converse is true. There are many good big-boat sailors who don't do well in small boats. A big, heavy boat covers up a lot of mistakes for you, but they exist, they're there. You can make a mistake in a 12-Meter, being a little slow to react to a puff, for example, and hardly anyone will notice it. In a dinghy, the rescue boat will notice it and come pull you out of the water. That's why it's good to learn to sail in a dinghy or its equivalent, where mistakes are obvious. We brought small-boat sailing concepts to *Weatherly* and they worked.

All three of my boys sail. The two older ones, Trip and Bruce, have

Dinghy sailing, according to Mosbacher, helps develop the skills used in 12-Meter sailing.

done a great deal of it. I've tried to help by responding, within reason, to anything they want. That means assistance in getting a boat and tuning it, and answering questions. I've made a conscious effort not to volunteer very much. There have been too many sailing fathers who have been on their sons' backs. Some of the sons are among our finest sailors, but I have always felt that a few of these kids didn't really enjoy it very much—maybe they did, but they didn't seem to.

If my boys want to sail—and I know the two older ones do and I think the third one does, although he hasn't made up his mind for sure —I'll do anything in the world to help them learn, but I don't want to push them. I sail with them, comment on their performances and on occasion after a race I'll ask them why in the world they did this or that. I don't watch them regularly for a variety of reasons—I don't want to be a Little-League father to them.

They have done well on their own. Trip missed the better part of the '67 and '68 seasons because of an operation and an accident, so he's been held up a bit in his development as a sailor, but he's a good one. Bruce is a fine sailor—as a Midget in 1967, he was in six regattas and won them all. He did not go to the Midget Championships. The only series he lost was in the Club eliminations, where he was beaten by another lad who went to the Midgets.

Both the older boys have done well with their Lightnings. My third son, John, has a Blue Jay. He managed to win the first regatta he entered. I also took him to Centerport, N.Y., in 1968 and he was third in a division of about thirty-five or forty boats. He could be a good sailor if he wants to be, but he hasn't made that decision yet.

I've kidded a lot with the boys about the various kinds of sailing they might do. They could sail anything from Finns to cruising boats. So far, they have had a great deal of fun doing a little bit of everything. They like sailing on cruising boats. They enjoy the companionship of a bigger boat and are anxious to learn about navigation and marlinspike seamanship, which is almost a lost art today. I think they like the idea of sailing the Finns because they can sail competitively at the drop of a hat without worrying about getting a crew.

Unfortunately, the notoriety inevitably involved in sailing 12-Meter boats has made it a little difficult for the boys. They have to mind their P's and Q's a lot more than some of the other kids who can get away with a certain amount of misbehavior and sloppy sailing. This is rough on them, but they take it pretty much in their stride. I think both the older boys have had some disappointments. There were some things in their field they might have been selected to do, but they weren't chosen because it might have been interpreted as favoritism. It's been a little tough on them but they've never said a word to me about it.

Actually, I'm quite happy about the kids. The only thing I regret was a mistake I made which caused Trip to miss seeing *Intrepid* in the Cup Races. He was manager of the football team at Choate, and the coach had told him he could stay in Newport a couple of extra days to see some races. I didn't understand this and I told him he had undertaken the responsibility of managing the football team and that's where he belonged. So I sent him back to Choate and he didn't see a race. Maybe that can be made up to him some day.

Once you get involved in sailing a candidate for the defense of the

BUS
MOSBACHER
Cup, your customary family living pattern is changed completely. It takes a tremendous amount of time from home and from business. It is a major effort that assumes priority over everything else. Pat and the boys and I think a great deal of the America's Cup and the tradition behind it, and we've felt considerable pride in being associated with *Weatherly* and *Intrepid*. As a family, we feel the effort and the pressures it puts on everyone is worth it.

However, these campaigns add a great deal of work to Pat's schedule. She has to run our own house in White Plains and has the ultimate responsibility for running the crew's quarters in Newport. At Eastbourne in '67, she had lots of help from Mrs. Gifford, our housekeeper, and some of the wives in our group, but she had to supervise the operation of a household of some thirty people and half a dozen in help. Fortunately, Pat's very capable. She's bright, she's not lazy, and she enjoys the whole operation enough so that she doesn't mind putting out the extra effort. At the same time, she manages to keep up her work as a member of a hospital board and all the other activities most women are engaged in. It takes a willing and understanding wife to help you take part in one of these things.

BIZZY MONTE-SANO: We had a great time at Eastbourne Lodge. In the morning there was always a rush for the newspapers that were piled on a table outside the dining room. We quickly scanned the stories about our activities of the day before. Woe be to any one of our group that was quoted in the press. We made his life miserable. And, of course, we

Pat Mosbacher, who shared her husband's tensions as well as his triumphs, was the First Lady of Eastbourne Lodge.

sniped at Bus more than anybody else. There was a lot of lighthearted nonsense.

Someone said the atmosphere at the Lodge was like that of a French château serving as headquarters for World War I flyers. There was fun and frivolity before the dawn patrols but behind it all was a deadly serious objective.

BUS MOSBACHER: One of the important things in sailing a 12-Meter is the degree of command entrusted to you by the owner or syndicate. In 1958, on *Vim* I was the assistant helmsman. About ten minutes before each start, I was invited to take the wheel. Don Matthews was skipper of *Vim* and he was in charge, but once he turned the wheel over to me, he never exercised the prerogatives of command.

When Henry Mercer asked me to sail *Weatherly* in '62, I said, "Only under certain conditions." I said I felt like a spoiled brat in a way and I didn't mean to be—I didn't want to say, "It's got to be my ball and bat or I won't play," but that's what it sounded like and I guess that's what I really meant. I said I hoped I wouldn't be unreasonable about anything but I had to have a free hand. Mr. Mercer agreed completely, and I've always thought that was perhaps because he was in the shipping business and very likely let his captains run their ships.

Now, this was again clearly spelled out when we started talking about *Intrepid*. I welcomed the opportunity of working with Olin, but as far as sailing the boat was concerned, I didn't feel it was worth the great time and effort unless I was given a free hand. I didn't think we had the time to have a board meeting whenever I felt I needed a new jib or spinnaker. And, of course, the Syndicate concurred and my relationship with them was simply wonderful.

TOBY TOBIN: In the spring of '67, shortly after *Intrepid* was launched, I sensed an undercurrent of feeling among the crew about who was in overall charge of the boat: Bus or Sparkman & Stephens. Between practice sessions, Sparkman & Stephens had the foot of the mast moved

The famous grin was never broader than on the day Mosbacher won the third race from **Gretel** *to take a two-to-one lead over the Australians in the 1962 Cup Races.*

141

aft and had ballast added without consulting Bus. I knew the situation couldn't last because Bus wouldn't tolerate it and because the people concerned were too mature to let such things disrupt a major team effort. Shortly thereafter, the crew really took charge and began removing extra-weight items such as the lower backstays and the forward steering wheel.

VIC ROMAGNA: Bus is one of the most dedicated racing men in the sport. A group of people came along and handed him a machine that cost a great deal of money. They were intent on defending the America's Cup, which was very dear to them and to the New York Yacht Club. To Bus, this was a serious responsibility. Consequently, he wouldn't go out with a boat that could be improved in any way—it had to be at its peak.

BIZZY MONTE-SANO: Bus has the ability to recognize and respect excellence in others. Bus recognized Teddy Hood's great skill and was willing to go along with any decision Teddy made about sails. If Teddy thought a sail should be recut, Bus would follow his advice. As a result we had excellent sails. They contributed a great deal to *Intrepid's* speed. All you had to do was look at *Dame Pattie's* sails and realize how good ours were. They were terrific, absolutely.

BOBBY CONNELL: I think the Australians had a philosophy: build them a boat and they would sail it the best they could. In America, we would build a boat and if it wasn't the best boat possible, we'd change it. The Aussies sort of made do with what they had. Individually, they were extremely good sailors—they were probably tougher than we were. But they didn't have the sophistication, if that's what you'd call it. We did everything the easiest and fastest way possible.

BUS MOSBACHER: Some people, especially my dad, have said I'm very serious. If so, I'm not personally conscious of it, although I guess I have a fairly positive approach to things. When we were first married, Pat kidded me about the fact that some people liked to put the top back on the toothpaste and some didn't. I happen to be one of the ones that did.

Either you like to be organized or you don't. I like to be and, fortunately for *Intrepid,* so did Vic Romagna. We believe in being on time and in having people in specific places executing orderly, planned routines. Over the years we've worked out many systems, and Vic has really done the lion's share of translating ideas into organizational plans. I have never made a specific time-and-motion study of the way we planned things on *Intrepid,* but, in essence, that's what you do when you set up an operation plan for a 12-Meter boat—you might call it the choreography of racing. You have *X* number of men who have to do certain jobs with split-second timing. They must do them as fast and as well as possible to eliminate any chance of a foul-up. Organizing, first the physical layout and then the people, is a fascinating study.

With *Intrepid* we had the mock-up of the deck layout and we had to go through the motions of grinding the winches, tailing the drums, and casting off. We had to visualize where jib-sheet leads would be and where the slapping wires were. Obviously, you can't put a man's face just forward of a jib-sheet block. Everything has to be worked out to get the most efficiency with the minimum of hazards. The only way to do this is to go through every operation yourself. I'm not much of a winch grinder and not a good tailer but I had to go through the motions to know what was involved. Then, you have to watch the crew members in every operation—not so much to look over their shoulders for mistakes as to make sure there isn't a better way to do the job.

The skipper has to know the location and function of every last item on the boat. You also have to know to the second what every crew member is doing on any maneuver, whether it's tacking, jibing, or changing sails. Most important is knowing your men and what you can expect of them. The *Intrepid* crew were great, but I couldn't ask them to walk on water. We did demand a great deal of them and they responded wonderfully, but you have to know how far to go with them.

TOBY TOBIN: On *Intrepid,* the crew was connected to the skipper the way marionettes are connected to their operator. There was more to it than that, obviously. Bus was more totally in control of everything that happened on his vessel than anyone I've ever sailed with: he was concerned with the angle and size and particularly the weight of the cleat used on the spinnaker downhaul; he was concerned with where I kept my pencils and erasers for navigation—nothing happened on that boat that he wasn't intimately concerned with. Underway, unless Bus said something, we never changed trim or did anything that was not part of an established maneuver. He made it clear early in the season that there would be a set drill for everything, and we stuck rigidly to the established systems unless or until it was decided that there was good reason to change them.

At the beginning of the '67 season, we were putting on a jib; when you hank it on on a cruising boat, you normally secure the tack and hank it on and pull it up. Bus made it clear that wasn't the way you did

Intrepid's skipper was a stickler for organization. Each crew member was expected to maintain his gear in perfect working order, so all hands turned to on days in port.

TOBY TOBIN it on a 12-Meter. You attached the head and pulled the jib up as you hanked it on. His total control and his willingness to expend the time and energy to become familiar with every screw on board was what made him so good.

DAVE ELWELL: When you sailed with Bus, if you were winning by five minutes, you wanted to try like hell to win by ten minutes. Some people think you win a race as long as you get there first, and maybe that's what counts as far as numbers are concerned. But Bus instilled in us the feeling that there was more to winning a race than being first. It was how you went about it.

BOBBY CONNELL: Bus knew what he wanted and you knew he was going to get it whether it came from you or not. Anyone who gave him the performance he wanted got recognized for it. He let you know when you did a great job or what you were doing wrong and how to change it so you could do even better.

BILL STRAWBRIDGE: When Bus was standing in the cockpit steering the *Intrepid,* he knew exactly what every man was doing every minute and he could spot something going wrong almost before it happened. That was his great talent, aside from the fact he could sail the boat so damn well.

BIZZY MONTE-SANO: Bus was absolutely great because he realized that a boat needs not only excellent sailors but people who get on well together. It was like fitting a jigsaw puzzle together. If an individual was an excellent hand but was incapable of working with other people and unable to communicate or participate with the group as a whole, he wasn't the right man for the *Intrepid* crew. One of Bus's strong points was being able to assess people.

TOBY TOBIN: Bus was very conscious of the *Intrepid* family. He liked people to be together and in Newport he rarely went out for dinner or anywhere. He almost always ate with the crew and made a point of spending the evening with them. He usually went to bed pretty early. His peculiar vice was an intense desire for "awful-awfuls." That was the name for the milkshakes we used to get with Bus almost every night at the ice cream store.

DAVE ELWELL: He was very demanding, but if you were out there to win boat races, Bus was without doubt the guy to sail with. I respected him as a sailor and as a person. He was a good sailor and a good friend and you wanted to please him on both counts. And, somehow, you developed some pretty high standards of your own that you wanted to live up to.

There were a lot of things we did besides just sailing the boat. When we got off we went swimming with Bus and things like that, which were every bit as important to me as the sailing.

BUS MOSBACHER: Knowing the physical capacities of your crew was one thing, but understanding their personalities was equally important. We were a closely knit group, living under one roof most of the time, and I tried to become attuned to the diverse temperaments of the crew.

TOBY TOBIN: One day in Buzzards Bay I misread my plot and gave Bus the wrong course. I misread it by 10° and we sailed for two or three miles on the wrong heading. I wasn't happy to report to Bus when I discovered the mistake, and he knew it. His response was kinder than I think mine might have been. All he said was, "Well, Toby, it's nice to know you're human."

BIZZY MONTE-SANO: I remember our first race with *Columbia* because it was July eighth, my birthday. We were worried about her because she seemed fast in light air, and Bus thought she might be every bit our equal or even better in the wind we had that day. So he was very aggressive at the starting line, and when the gun went off we were headed away from the starting line with Briggs Cunningham tucked away so he had no place to go. When we rounded up and came back to the line, he was dead behind us and we were sitting on his wind. *Columbia* crossed the line about twenty seconds astern of us. Bus looked at her and then looked at me and said, "That's your birthday present." Well, it couldn't have been a better present. Watching Bus do that was one of the most exciting moments of the whole summer.

BOBBY CONNELL: When Bus made his regular head call on the leeward leg, he came below and talked with us about how things were going, and he kidded a bit about staying out the night before or something like that. He knew what was happening and about the social activity of the crew. I don't know how he knew, but when we were out he knew it.

BUS MOSBACHER: There were times during the summer when decision-

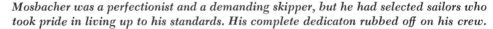

Mosbacher was a perfectionist and a demanding skipper, but he had selected sailors who took pride in living up to his standards. His complete dedicaton rubbed off on his crew.

making was difficult. I was a little embarrassed when I asked Victor to give up the navigator's job after I had really begged him to take it. Eventually, it was clear the job wasn't getting the attention it needed. That wasn't his fault; it was mine. Vic didn't want the job and he took it only as a favor to me because, at the time, I didn't think there was anyone else who could do it.

I thought the measurement incident was most unfortunate in every sense of the word, especially the way it was handled by *Dame Pattie's* designer, Warwick Hood, and, indirectly, by Jock Sturrock. It was so unnecessary. We stripped *Intrepid* for the so-called light measurement [1] just as we've done in this country since 1958. When we were sailing *Vim* in the trials in '58, we were surprised at the way the rule was interpreted—it was somewhat nebulous about what you took off and what you left on the boat for the light measurement. The rule said you should have a mainsail and jib, but everyone used a spinnaker staysail for the jib. It was acceptable under the rule and we became accustomed to doing it that way.

In '67, *Intrepid* was measured after *Dame Pattie*. We floated well on our lines. Warwick Hood and Olin were in the small boat with Bob Blumenstock who did the measuring. Hood was grumbling about something and was obviously upset. So after the measuring, I asked Olin to talk with Hood, find out what was bothering him, and explain that the removal of winches and equipment was according to the accepted interpretation of the rule. I also said that if Hood had some objections, we would put some gear back aboard *Intrepid* or, if he wanted to remove some equipment from *Dame Pattie*, Bob Blumenstock would probably be glad to refloat her.

Warwick Hood said he wanted to think about it, and that was the end of the conversation. I took *Intrepid* out for a practice sail. When we came in, we were greeted at the dock by ten or twelve members of the press. From them I gathered that Hood had gone to Commodore Morgan and registered a formal protest with the America's Cup Committee. The word was that *Intrepid* had been improperly measured and that we were to be remeasured. That sent my blood pressure to the roof. As I interpreted the information, Hood said that we had cheated and had made a public issue of it. Also, he had not had the decency to respond when we had tried to keep the matter on a reasonable and orderly discussion basis. There had been no effort on our part to hide anything or to cheat. I thought we had bent over backwards to be fair, and to be treated in such a cavalier manner by Hood was a little more than I could take. In addition, I couldn't understand why the captain of *Dame*

[1] Under 12-Meter rules, a boat is measured in standard (light) condition without crew and with a limited amount of sails and equipment. In this condition, the boat should float at the bottom of the triangular measurement marks on the hull. She is then measured in sailing condition with crew and all equipment and she should float at the top—but not over—the measurement marks.

Pattie, a man I thought I had known fairly well and had considered a friend for five or six years, hadn't had the courtesy to discuss the problem with me face to face. If he had, there wouldn't have been any excitement as far as I was concerned.

I didn't think anything relating to the rules should be agreed upon privately, but there was nothing secret about this situation. With everyone's full knowledge, we were trying to come to an agreement about the vague part of the measurement rule. We had had a similar experience with Allen Payne in 1962, when we thought the Australians were doing something that wasn't correct. We pointed it out to Payne, discussed the rule thoroughly, and that was the end of it.

We insisted that if we were to be remeasured, *Dame Pattie* should be also. Sturrock said Hood wouldn't agree to this but he would. So both boats were refloated and remeasured. There was no change. When we put on the fairing blocks they wanted, they added some twenty or thirty pounds. *Intrepid* was not heavy at any time.

There were some people who considered the incident a ploy and said, Don't let it upset you. But the crew was pretty annoyed that we had to waste a full day getting remeasured. We didn't enjoy being towed up to the hurricane hole at the Destroyer Base in a hard northwester that got us soaking wet, and it certainly didn't help to see half the Australian crew eating our lunch while we were getting *Intrepid* measured. Jock and Warwick Hood and half a dozen of them rode up to the measuring place on our tender, *Mary Poppins,* and sat there consuming our lunch. We had had nothing to eat, and while we weren't about to starve to death, it was another turn of the screw.

A few days later I met with Jock and I told him he was captain of his boat and whether he was responsible for the incident or not, it was damned poor of him not to call me or see me and discuss what was going on. He knew how I felt and I still feel that way.

Jock indicated that he regretted the situation very much but he also led me to believe that he was not a free agent in this area.

Because the Cup races had national and international connotations, I felt great pressure to keep everything on a high level of sportsmanship. I thought it was too bad when something upset this. I don't know whether it was gamesmanship; maybe it was. I was an easy mark for someone who wanted to play that game. Maybe the whole point was to get my goat. If that was the purpose, it succeeded one thousand per cent. I felt that I had virtually been called a liar publicly, and I didn't like that or the people who did it. On the other hand, after the series was over Olin had Hood up to his house for the weekend. So Olin was a far more forgiving guy than I was, I guess.

BILL STRAWBRIDGE: After the measurement incident, I was invited to a cocktail party by the Australian Chargé d'Affaires, who was in Newport for the races. As soon as I arrived I realized the purpose of the party was for me to meet and talk with the head of the Australian Syndicate so we could at least keep this fracas from getting out of our respective houses. After the party I went to Eastbourne Lodge to talk with Bus and Olin. I explained to Bus about my conversation with the Australians and that everyone wanted to let the measurement incident cool off and forget about it.

Bus somehow got the idea that I had come from the Aussies with an apology, which he felt he should have received from Jock Sturrock. The apology story got to the press and the Australian correspondents quickly filed stories with their papers. I spoke with some of the American newspapermen and explained the situation, which was a misunderstanding and not a news story. As far as I can remember nothing appeared in the papers here. Subsequently, George O'Day arranged a meeting between Bus and Jock in a drugstore and then later on the schooner *America*. They were photographed smiling and shaking hands, and that more or less closed the incident as far as the press was concerned.

BUS MOSBACHER: When you campaign a 12-Meter, there is no letup from the pressure. We had a great boat in *Intrepid,* but that didn't make life any easier. For me, that just increased the pressure because there was no excuse for not winning. So I had to keep pushing all the time. I never forgot for a moment that two masts had come down alongside of me. Once in a while my patience wore thin—and it shouldn't have. So I got mad when someone wanted to remeasure us when there was no reason for it, and I blew my top when *Eagle* gave that spinnaker to *Columbia.* Sometimes at night I walked up and down in my bedroom saying, "It's only a game; it's only a sport. It's only a game."

GEORGE O'DAY: Bus is a tough leader and he was harder to work with in '67 than he was in '62. He was more short-tempered and he couldn't tolerate as much. This is not an easy sport. A lot of people think sailing a Twelve is easy, but not the way Bus does it.

BUS MOSBACHER: During the summer at Newport, two unique incidents made me realize more than ever the tremendous interest generated by the America's Cup Races. One was a letter from the men on the United States aircraft carrier *Intrepid,* the other was a visit from the King of Greece.

Just before the conclusion of the final trials I received a letter from Commander Thomas Brown, USN, Executive Officer of the carrier. The letter said in part:

> "The officers and men of the aircraft carrier *USS Intrepid,* now deployed on 'Yankee Station' in the Gulf of Tonkin, have been watching your qualifying races closely and enthusiastically. You can be assured that you have 3,200 'Fighting I' INTREPID men on this side of the world rooting for your success.
>
> "We would appreciate a copy of your victories and your projected schedule so that we can continue following *Intrepid's* progress. Above all, we particularly hope that you make the finals and represent the U.S. against the Australian challenger. As soon as the American entry is chosen, we would appreciate hearing from you.
>
> "We'll continue upholding *Intrepid's* name here at the Tonkin Gulf Yacht Club and hope you do the same during your forthcoming races."

This word from Vietnam meant a great deal to me and our crew. Through some friends at the Newport Naval Base I sent a cable to Commander Brown: "Your enthusiastic support was reflected in our performance in the trials which resulted in the selection of your namesake today as the defender of the America's Cup. We will endeavor to maintain the same fighting spirit you have on board *Intrepid* on 'Yankee Station.' Our warmest wishes to you and all INTREPID men on board."

The visit from King Constantine was partially the result of a trip Pat and I, the George Hinmans, and the senior Monte-Sanos had taken to Greece a couple of years before. Bob Bavier, who knew the King through the International Yacht Racing Union, had written ahead, and when we arrived in Greece we were invited for dinner and then for sailing the next day. The King, an Olympic Gold Medal winner, proposed a race in Dragons. Instead of sailing against him, I thought the better part of valor would be to sail with him, which I did. It was a delightful experience and provided the basis for a lasting friendship.

During the sail, I attempted to trim the spinnaker, but found the sheet wouldn't budge. I discovered the King was sitting on the line and I quietly asked him how I should ask a King to move. "Tell him to get his — off the sheet," he said. That was the kind of day it was.

For some time the King had been contemplating a Greek challenge for the America's Cup. One of the purposes of his private visit to this country was to explore the possibilities of a challenge and to familiarize himself with 12-Meter yachts. The King had planned for months to come and sail on the Twelves with us. He had originally hoped to live with our crew at Eastbourne Lodge, but for a variety of reasons plans were changed so that the King and Queen came to Newport as the guests of Wiley Buchanan. The morning after his arrival he showed up at Eastbourne Lodge at 7:30 a.m. for breakfast. He wore a white turtleneck sweater and slacks and looked like any well-groomed yachtsman in Newport for the races—except for a sizable entourage of federal agents and state and local police.

Over coffee we chatted about *Intrepid* and her capabilities and then went down to the Newport Shipyard where the boat was hauled out for a final polishing before the Cup Races. The King, or "K.C." as our boys irreverently called him, followed me up the ladder onto *Intrepid* and spent more than an hour scrutinizing the boat above and below decks. He asked a lot of questions. His knowledge and his curiosity were remarkable.

I had suggested that we go for a sail on *Constellation,* but by that time the weather had deteriorated. There were heavy rain squalls and winds gusting around twenty knots, but the King wasn't going to pass up the opportunity. "Why not go out?" he said. "This isn't bad." We rounded up a reluctant crew and got *Connie* underway, much to the chagrin of the security forces, who followed with walkie-talkies in an admiral's gig borrowed from the Naval station. It was a rugged sail, but the King, at the wheel of a Twelve for the first time, had a ball.

"We returned in midafternoon and the King took off for Washington and an informal visit with President Johnson. He hurried back to Newport for the first Cup Race and followed it from our tender, *Mary Poppins.* The following morning he flew to Kennedy Airport and then to Greece. For us, his visit was a delightful interlude in the otherwise serious business of racing.

The Defense

8

BUS MOSBACHER: On the day of our first race with *Dame Pattie,* I must confess I was delighted to see we had a good solid breeze. I didn't know what the Challenger was going to be like, but I did know what *Intrepid* could do when it breezed up. We had no special strategy. I just wanted to get *Intrepid* on the line with clear wind and get her moving as fast as I could.

Jock made no attempt to mix it up at the start so we got away well to windward of him. We soon began to bother him, and he tacked away and we covered. Our sails looked fine and the boat went beautifully. We had him by almost two minutes at the mark.

TOBY TOBIN: After months and years of preparation, the hours of practice and the nights of worry, we finally found out. We beat *Dame Pattie* by six minutes in a fresh eighteen-to-twenty-knot easterly breeze. We absolutely killed them. They couldn't point or foot or tack with us, and their sail-handling was less competent, and their sails didn't hold up in the breeze. Our fantastic 7½-ounce main stood beautifully, their 12½-ounce lost shape until it seemed aback to the battens. They heeled much more than we did and were jolted by the seas.

Although we now felt quite cocky, we didn't before the race. Most of us were nervous and it showed in slightly forced comments, meticulous attention to obscure details, and by neglecting lunch.

At the start Bus declined to tangle and got a good weather berth

153

America's Cup Course Newport, R.I.

12 Meter Olympic Cup Course

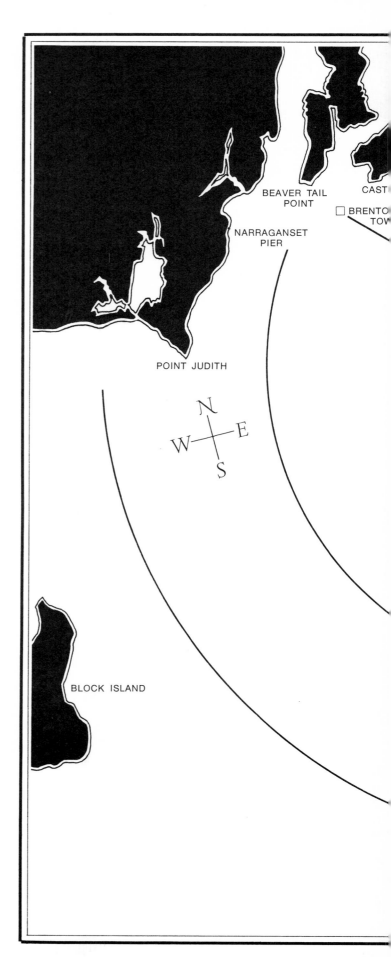

BEAVER TAIL
POINT

CAST

☐ BRENTO
TOW

NARRAGANSET
PIER

POINT JUDITH

N
W E
S

BLOCK ISLAND

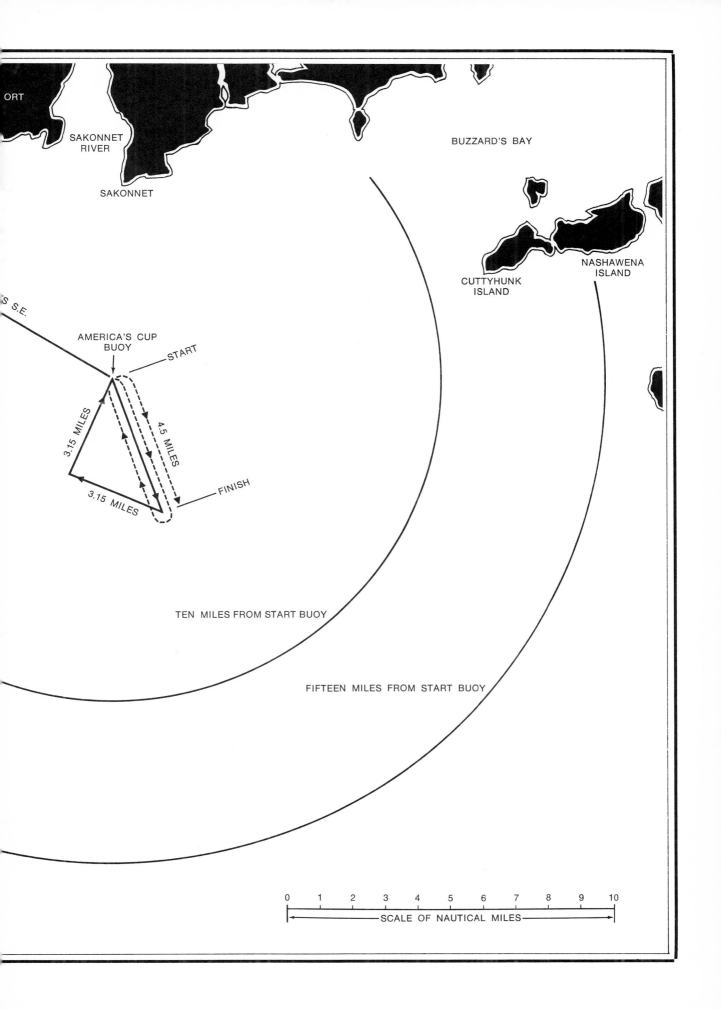

about even on the line with *Dame Pattie*. Twenty minutes later we had driven through Sturrock and he started a tacking duel. Despite the great speed of their trimming, we gained on each tack, seldom dropping our speed below seven knots and never below six. After five tacks, Jock saw they were losing and broke off the short tacking bit. In the clear cold easterly, we gained on every leg, but the windward legs were our best with gains of 1:50 on the first, 1:36 on the second and 0.42 on the third, when we deliberately eased off to save the rig for another day.

At the start of the first race in the twentieth match for the America's Cup, Intrepid *was slightly to weather and ten seconds behind* Dame Pattie.

The defender ate out to windward and Sturrock was forced to tack to clear his wind.

Mosbacher covered and that was the boat race. Pounding in the seas, the challenger was 1' 50" behind at the first mark and 5' 58" at the finish.

The Aussies sail handling was not as crisp as in '62. Here, Pattie's spinnaker got out of control.

BUS MOSBACHER: The morning of the second Cup Race it seemed like everyone got down to the boat early. They checked out the rigging and cleaned winches and did all the things they'd done all summer, except on that morning they did everything with a new kind of crisp assurance. I don't think I've seen a better crew.

We towed out to the starting line. It wasn't as wet as the day before. The wind was still out of the east but not as strong. We decided to use the five-ounce jib. During the eleven-thirty sandwich break, the boys were needling each other about how they'd better not foul up anything because there were plenty of guys on *Constellation* that could take their places.

We put the main on and gave our tow line to *Mary Poppins*. I noticed *Dame Pattie's* mainsail looked a bit better. We went into the starting sequence. There was no pressure from Jock. We got on his weather quarter and crossed the line on starboard tack.

OLIN STEPHENS: Watching the start, I don't know whether *Dame Pattie* was closer winded boat-for-boat or whether it was simply her position that gave her a slight advantage. I presume Bus was thinking about the discussion we had about this situation if it should come up. In any case, he tacked away and Sturrock followed. This put Bus on his lee bow and it was only a matter of minutes before you could see *Intrepid* was footing enough faster so that all of *Dame Pattie's* pointing ability wasn't doing her much good. I don't suppose it was more than ten or twelve minutes, if I remember it, that both boats were on the port tack and *Intrepid* had worked far enough ahead to tack and cross *Dame Pattie's* bow comfortably. Then Bus tacked on her weather bow and you might say that was the boat race.

TOBY TOBIN: We beat the Aussies in the second race by three minutes and thirty-six seconds. It was less than the first day, but still a solid thrashing. The course was the same at 075 magnetic. Both boats were about even on the line at the start, with *Intrepid* to windward. In the light air *Dame Pattie* was able to squeeze up under us and forced us to tack about five minutes after the start. She followed, but Bus drove *Intrepid* off a bit, building up her speed, and after another ten minutes we were able to tack back across her bow. Sturrock started a tacking duel in which we gained, especially when he tried a false tack which we caught, and picked up a couple of boat lengths. We led by about a

At the start of the second race (photographs A–D), the two boats hit the line evenly. Sturrock was to leeward, squeezing up on **Intrepid.**

A

TOBY
TOBIN

minute at the windward mark. With a fine spinnaker set and jibe on the two leeward legs we gained another minute.

Since the wind seemed to have breezed up, we shifted to a nine-ounce genoa for the next weather leg. *Dame Pattie* used the same jib she had started with and, to our surprise, held us even up the leg. On the run both boats tacked downwind and we picked up a minute and a half. On the final windward leg, we only gained about ten seconds. Did we have on the wrong jib? Did they have a better combination or was the *Dame* fairly good in moderate air? Certainly the second and third windward legs must have given the Aussies some encouragement. With lighter air forecast, perhaps Jock would be more aggressive at the start. If he could nail us there, we might have trouble breaking clear.

B

Intrepid *tacked to get out of the backdraft and* Pattie *covered.*

Mosbacher, driving off, picked up speed for about ten minutes. Then he tacked . . .

C

D

. . . and crossed Sturrock comfortably.

One of the interesting tactical features of an America's Cup race is playing the slop kicked up by the spectator fleet. The Coast Guard patrol just can't keep the margins of the course clear and so a confused turbulent sea exists within three hundred yards of the edge. We felt we could withstand this condition better than the *Dame,* so we tried to work her into the rougher going.

On the day of the third race, the high pressure area was stationary with a tightening gradient and as hurricane Doria began to move towards us again, we had a brisk dry northeaster at fifteen to twenty knots with steep seas and long swells running ahead of the storm. The Aussies missed their guess if they were looking for light air. It's hard to figure why they wanted a moderate breeze when all summer they had seemed interested in heavy air.

We were surprised Jock didn't try anything aggressive at the start. The third race was similar to the second, with both boats about even on the line; Bus had us a couple or three lengths to windward. A remarkable example of *Intrepid's* windward ability occurred soon after the start. Both boats were headed about fifteen degrees, but instead of falling behind and into *Dame Pattie's* wind shadow, *Intrepid* climbed steadily ahead and out to windward until she had sailed around the challenger in spite of the header. We continued on this tack to the lay line, then tacked first, and *Pattie* followed suit.

At the beginning of the third race (photographs A–C), Mosbacher was in his favorite position.

A

B

Despite a 15° header, he worked to windward of Dame Pattie . . .

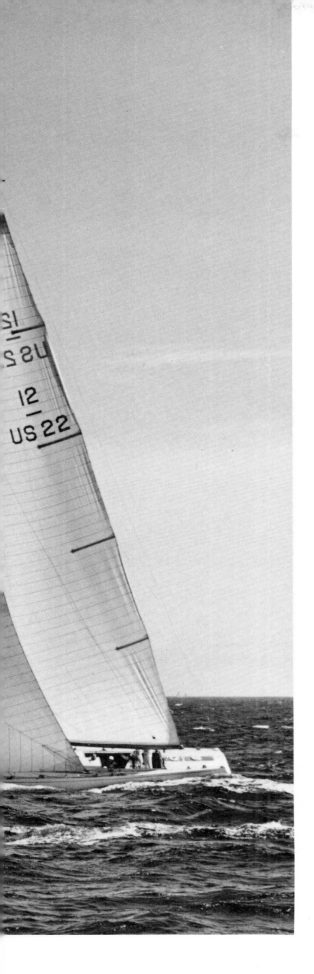

C

. . . and held on until he tacked on the layline.

TOBY
TOBIN

Then came a bizarre and awesome incident—a near collision between a Cup defender and a helicopter.

A Coast Guard chopper apparently was dispatched to chase off a small sailboat that was directly in our track. Hovering over it, the helicopter's tremendous downdraft capsized the boat. The patrol suddenly became a rescue mission and a line was lowered from the chopper to the occupants of the sailboat. The helicopter was headed into the wind and apparently unable to see us approaching, but we thought he could see us and naturally expected him to move. Instead, as we got in close, he abruptly backed down on us and had our sails aback before we could bear off to go around him. It was frightening, but everyone on *Intrepid* was thinking more about the boat and the rig than themselves.

We had been reluctant to change course because we were on the layline, but after bearing off and getting a ten degree header, we had to tack to get around the mark. In spite of our detour we had the *Dame* by a minute and twenty seconds. We held about even on the leeward legs although our set, jibe, and take-down all seemed better than theirs. We felt they had a very poor leeward rounding—chute down way early and very overtrimmed on their approach to the mark.

On both the second and third windward legs we gained significantly, not as much as in the first race, but enough to lead by four minutes and forty-one seconds at the finish.

Attempting to clear the first leg of the course a Coast Guard helicopter blew over a Beatle catboat and then had to rescue the occupants. The chopper was right on the layline and Mosbacher was reluctant to change course. Finally, as the helicopter lifted off and came back at him, he bore off abruptly as Intrepid *felt the blast of the downdraft. Despite the incident and a header which forced Mosbacher to tack to cover* Dame Pattie, *the Defender led by 1′ 21″ at the mark.*

Dame Pattie *didn't stand up well in the fifteen-knot breeze. She heeled well over and took a lot of water.*

Dame Pattie looked to us like a wounded bird. She heeled way over, her mast fell off to leeward excessively, her mainsail was aback, and she pitched awkwardly in the seas and seemed to slide to leeward with each successive plunge. Surely one of *Intrepid's* advantages was Bus's delicate touch on the wheel in the rough going, but the boat itself deserves much credit for the way it kept going in the slop. Even in a series of waves which you would expect to knock her down two or three knots, she went only from 7.8 to 7.5 knots.

GEORGE O'DAY: During the third race we had that thing with the helicopter. I guess I noticed it when we were about a mile away. So I said to Bus, "Look, there's a little boat out there with a helicopter over it." We kept driving up to it and I said, "Bus, it's right in line, it's right on our course," but he kept going and going. And I said, "Bus, you gotta watch out, you don't know what's going to happen when you get into that air turbulence. Finally, both Vic and I yelled at Bus and said, "For God's sake, he's backing down!" and then Bus spun the wheel, and that's when the chopper started to lift off. Bus didn't realize that they don't always take off forwards like a plane.

VIC ROMAGNA: When the helicopter came along I was on the mainsheet and when we had to bear off, I let the sheet go because Bus couldn't head down with it trimmed. George was so intent on watching the helicopter he didn't take the preventer turns off the lee backstay so the boom hit the backstay and wouldn't go off. And I said, "Christ sake, George, get the backstay off," and he finally did. Then Bus said, "God damn it George, you're going to be on *Constellation* yet." Bus doesn't remember saying it, but he laughed like the dickens when we told him afterward.

We kept going toward the helicopter because we didn't know he was rescuing people, we didn't know he had blown the boat over. He shouldn't have been there in the first place. We kept going because we were on the layline for the windward mark.

BUS MOSBACHER: After we tacked for the mark, I think it was George who spotted the helicopter with a small sailboat under it. Everybody looked and nobody could see the sailboat. There were whitecaps and we thought possibly George had seen a whitecap under the helicopter. We didn't know what it was doing there. As we approached, we saw that it was some kind of rescue operation, because the wire was being lowered from the helicopter with a belt or whatever it is. We got closer and closer and could see there was a boat. I kept hoping that the progress of the rescue was such that the chopper would be up and out of the way before we got there, but as we came closer, it was obvious that either she wasn't going to move out of the way or wasn't able to, so at the last minute I swung to leeward of the helicopter.

I'd never been in a helicopter, but I assumed that it took off into the wind like an airplane. I thought that if I swung around under her stern I would be in pretty good shape. As we got there and eased off, we forgot to let go our backstay. The mainsail could have been badly ripped or even broken the boom.

We swung to go under her stern and she did start to take off, but she started going backwards. This brought her much closer than I had any idea she would come and as she backed down on us we were all scared to death, but we were delighted when it was all over almost before it started.

Because we had to bear off and because of a header, we had to tack to cover *Dame Pattie,* who had climbed up on our port quarter. Fortunately, we still had her, so it wasn't fatal. I don't think I would sail a boat that close to a helicopter again if I had any option in the matter. I didn't realize the downdraft would be such a blast until we got there.

TOBY TOBIN: Following the third race, *Dame Pattie* flew the "negative" flag when the Race Committee inquired if they would race the next day. The layday gave us a chance to dry out sails and the boat after the very wet third race. But when threats of hurricane Doria forced another postponement, we began to fidget and tried to think up some busy-work to occupy our idle hands.

Dame Pattie's *crew. Jock Sturrock, standing, wears a yachting cap. On his left is the navigator, Norm Wright.*

The following day the Race Committee ordered the yachts to
"stand by" while the fog hovered so thick we couldn't even see Goat
Island. By ten-thirty the harbor was clear, and we got underway eager to
finish the series. At the mouth of the harbor we hit a dense wall of fog
and stopped and circled nervously in the midst of Sunday's spectator
fleet. Finally, when there was no hope of starting a race within the
specified time limits the Committee called it off for yet another day.

Monday was as misty as Sunday but the Race Committee sent us out
in spite of the heavy fog en route. Everyone with radar had it working.
When we got to the Cup buoy, the fog was so thick we couldn't see our
towboat, but it was spotty, and as the day wore on it showed signs of
clearing. Finally, at 14:10, ten minutes before the time limit, the Committee started the fourth race. It seemed a little wild, because the fog
was dense at the start, but half an hour later we had three-mile visibility.

At the start Jock tangled with Bus for the first time. We nearly forced
him over early by coming up underneath him but he tacked clear and
the yachts started on opposite tacks with *Intrepid* well to weather. We
tacked back to cover Jock and both boats continued out on starboard
tack. *Dame Pattie* tried to squeeze up beneath us, hoping to give us
some backwind, but we sailed by her to windward, forcing her to tack
beneath us.

Jock then started a tacking duel, the first move of which was well
executed. As soon as we covered him, he came up as if to tack and Bus
put *Intrepid's* helm down to cover. But he moved too quickly and
Intrepid's genoa was aback before we realized *Dame Pattie* was trying a
false tack and was falling off on port tack again. We were able to fall off
with him, but our speed suffered. *Intrepid* gained steadily on the next
few tacks and Jock soon gave up this strategy.

The remainder of the race had a familiar pattern: significant gains on
the windward legs and slight gains on the reaching legs. But on the run
they picked up on us dramatically. They seemed to carry a better breeze
and chopped our lead by a third. We took two extra jibes to stay
between them and the mark. We continued to gain on the final windward leg and crossed the finish line with a lead of three minutes and
thirty-five seconds.

The final gun produced mixed emotions: elation at victory, disappointment that the challenge had not been more challenging, and the
bittersweet sentiment that a long summer of dedication had reached its
end.

Shortly after the start of the fourth race Sturrock initiated a tacking duel (photographs A–B).

A

B

Intrepid *covered and* Dame Pattie *flipped over onto port tack.*

Mosbacher held on and then tacked to windward of the challenger. Unable to gain, the Aussies broke off the quick tacking ploy. Intrepid had a lead of 1′ 35″ at the windward mark.

TOBY
TOBIN
The champagne I had secretly stored below on the previous day was broken out immediately after the finish, still cold through some unexplained thermal mystery. We toasted our opponents, who responded with cheers. They flew the "negative" flag again, not in resignation but as a token of sportsmanship that recognized the match was over and no further races were necessary.

As the successful defender slides past the Race Committee boat, she is saluted by Committeemen.

174

Intrepid *won the fourth and final race by 3' 35'' and after the finish both boats exchanged cheers. With good-humored sportsmanship, Dame Pattie's crew acknowledged defeat by flying the "negative" flag, meaning no race tomorrow.*

Champagne is broken out to celebrate the triumph.

It was almost twilight when Mary Poppins *eased the Cup Defender into her Newport Shipyard slip.*

TOBY
TOBIN

On the way in the two boats came close together between the jets of welcoming fireboats and Bus invited all the Australian crew to Eastbourne Lodge to join in our party.

Our arrival in Newport produced a spine-tingling din and our own docking touched off some good-natured boisterousness. Starting with Bus, every member of the crew was wrestled overboard and when the Race Committee arrived to congratulate us, a number of them were dunked too. Amid the glare of lights set up for TV camera crews, a number of other distinguished yachtsmen also got the deep six, which they seemed to enjoy as much as we did.

In the dockside victory celebration, Mosbacher was the first one wrestled into the drink. Strawbridge looks on, gleefully unaware that his turn is soon to come.

The skipper points an accusing finger as O'Day lands in the harbor.

*One Race Official got
too close to the action.*

TOBY
TOBINBack at Eastbourne, the celebration was already underway, and it kept going until the early hours. Most members of the Syndicate, including Mr. Vanderbilt, came in to share in the excitement. It was noisy and gay, so much so that at one point the tolerant Newport police requested us to cool it because neighbors were complaining.

By noon the next day three quarters of the crew were gone, the house deserted, *Intrepid* alone at the dock, and the waterfront abandoned.

Following the final race, Bob Bavier, skipper of the 1964 defender Constellation, *is moderator of the press conference at Newport Armory. Mosbacher is on his left and Sturrock on his right.*

Looking none the worse for his dunking, Mosbacher faces the TV cameras with Jock Sturrock.

BUS MOSBACHER: It is very hard to describe just how I felt when it was all over. There was a sense of satisfaction in having accomplished what we set out to do in the best way we knew how. This was strictly a team effort and that meant not only our crew but Olin and Straw and Teddy Hood, the Syndicate members and people like Paul Coble, the Syndicate's marine construction supervisor, and Chuck Saddler, our marine technician. And, of course, there was a great sense of relief, not so much from the physical strain, which is something, but from the great pressure of responsibility. The fact that we had a fine boat didn't lighten the load. No one on *Intrepid* let down for an instant until that last race was over.

I think *Dame Pattie* was a good boat, quite a good boat. Her construction perhaps was not equivalent to ours, but she seemed to go well in light air and the lower speed ranges. Possibly she could have gone

The challenger's layout was similar to Constellation's *but lacked the simple efficiency of* Intrepid's *deck plan. The American sails were generally lighter in weight but held their shape better. Mosbacher's crew was a cut above the Aussie's, and all these little differences added up to a few more seconds per mile.*

better in the stronger breezes than she did. I feel we would have been fortunate to win those races by a minute and a half instead of by larger margins.

I don't know why they trimmed her sails the way they did. It's quite different from what we would think proper under the conditions we had. Jock certainly didn't trim the boat the way he did *Gretel* in '62. In that series I think *Gretel* was even modified so they could make more efficient use of her traveler. But *Dame Pattie* seemed to have her traveler trimmed amidships and the mainsail strapped in very flat. I think the boat was overtrimmed, pointed very high, and sailed very close. I would have thought when she seemed so tender in the wind and seas we had, they would have set her traveler out to its maximum limits. That's what we did with *Weatherly* in '62, because she also was very tender and needed the traveler out so she could stand up and go. *Intrepid,* of course, was a very stable boat and we seldom had our traveler move more than ten to fourteen inches.

Dame Pattie's sails were not as good as ours and they didn't stand up well when it blew. Their crew work was good, but ours was better. Our tacking and spinnaker sets were considerably better, which surprised me because I have great respect for some of those Australian boys I've known for a long time. I don't really know what the problem was, but they certainly seemed less gung-ho than they were in '62.

I think it was Olin who summed things up in that very logical way of his. He said *Intrepid* was not a super-boat as some people seemed to think. She had a hull that was slightly faster upwind, her sails were a bit better, and the crew a shade sharper and that all added up to a successful defender.

It was a rare privilege to work closely with Olin and it was rewarding to see the dedication of the boys who worked on *Intrepid* and *Constellation*. They were never satisfied until things were just right. I enjoyed just being with a group of guys who were so uniquely motivated by the love of sailing. They all put out to the *n*th degree and that developed a sense of great cohesiveness among us. We achieved a degree of closeness and mutual respect that was intensely stimulating.

Even when *Vim* failed to be selected in '58, I looked back on that happily. Everyone on board had a feeling of satisfaction because they had given everything they had to give, and that was just as important to us as winning. The fact that *Intrepid* won put the icing on the cake, but the real reward was in the effort itself and in the sharing of the wonderfully close association with the superb *Intrepid* men and their ladies.

Appendix

CREW ROSTER

Intrepid

Emil Mosbacher, Jr.,
   Skipper

Robert A. Connell

David K. Elwell, Jr.

Edward C. Hall

George Hinman, Jr.

William E. Kelly

Vincent Monte-Sano, Jr.

George D. O'Day

Victor A. Romagna

Wallace E. Tobin

Samuel W. Wakeman

Constellation

Robert W. McCullough,
   Skipper

Leo H. Bombard, Jr.

Daniel P. Brown

John Browning

Richard duMoulin

David Rockefeller, Jr.

G. West Saltonstall

Gerald Y. Silverman

Norris Strawbridge

Richard Strawbridge

Thomas R. Young

A Note About the Editors

Robert W. Carrick has written widely on many subjects, but is perhaps best known as an authority on boats and boating. Born in New York City in 1913, Mr. Carrick was graduated from Williams College and during World War II was the commanding officer of a sub-chaser. He has worked with most of the major boating magazines and was co-founder and Managing Editor of the *Maine Coast Fisherman*. A consultant to the U.S. Department of Commerce, the Woods Hole Oceanographic Institute, and both the Grolier and Crowell-Collier Encyclopedias, he is the author of *The Pictorial History of the America's Cup Races* and the coauthor of *The Pictorial History of Outboard Motors*. Mr. Carrick lives and writes in Riverside, Connecticut.

Stanley Z. Rosenfeld, the world-famous yachting photographer, covered his first America's Cup Race in 1930 and has photographed every Cup Race since, continuing a tradition his father, Morris Rosenfeld, began in 1900. Born in New York in 1913, Mr. Rosenfeld attended New York University and commanded a landing craft in World War II. He is an active yachtsman, having raced in speedboats and sailing ocean racers. His photographs have appeared in magazines all over the world; he collaborated with his father on many yachting books, and was coauthor of *The Story of American Yachting*. When he's not out on the water, Mr. Rosenfeld lives in New York City.

A Note on the Type

The text of this book was set on the Linotype in a type face called Baskerville. The face is a facsimile reproduction of types cast from molds made for John Baskerville (1706–75) from his designs. The punches for the revived Linotype Baskerville were cut under the supervision of the English printer George W. Jones. John Baskerville's original face was one of the forerunners of the type style known as "modern face" to printers—a "modern" of the period A.D. 1800.
Composed by Kingsport Press, Inc., Kingsport, Tennessee
Printed by Universal Lithographers, Inc., Timonium, Maryland
Bound by L. H. Jenkins–Universal, Richmond, Virginia
Typography by David Paul